MYRACLES
& SECOND CHANCES

HOW SEVEN UNLIKELY PEOPLE ARE
REDEFINING THE MEANING OF FAMILY

KRIS SHINN
WITH BRANDI SHINN

Myracles & Second Chances:
How Seven Unlikely People are Redefining
the Meaning of Family

By Kris Shinn with Brandi Shinn

Copyright © June 2018
Above All Else, Inc.
PO Box 692
Greenbrier, AR 72058
501-679-5677
Info@aboveallelseservices.com

aboveallelseservices.com

Unless otherwise noted, all Scripture references are from the New King James Version of the Holy Bible. Published 1987 by Thomas Nelson Publishers. Used by permission.

ISBN: 978-0-692-14277-6

Printed in the United States of America

Dedicated to Garland Garrett.
He gave unselfishly to so many for so many years.
What an example for us to follow!

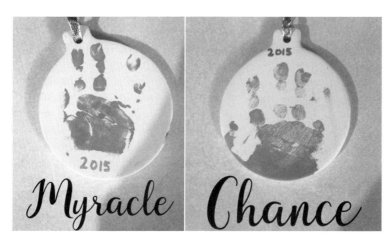

Handprints of Myracle and Chance Shinn

TABLE OF CONTENTS

FOREWORD

Myracles and Second Chances by Kris Shinn describes in down-to-earth terms how the journey of life encompasses many twists and turns. Success in life depends upon how we handle those gyrations, whether we are defeated or we rise to the occasion.

Miracles are interesting. Difficulty creates the need for one. An oyster creates a pearl by way of excruciating pain. In much the same way, the painful experiences of our lives provide opportunities for us to believe God for miracles. The Gospel of Mark chapter nine relates to us the story of a man who brought his son, who was experiencing seizures, to the disciples. The disciples were unable to cast out the spirit that had controlled the young man. The poor child foamed at the mouth and would throw himself into the water and fire. The constant around-the-clock care this boy required was no doubt taking a great toll on the family. Jesus appears on the scene and in desperation the man said to Jesus, "If you can do anything, please have compassion and heal my son." Jesus replied, "If you can believe, all things are possible to him who believes."

Kris and Brandi Shinn have earned the right to take on the subject of *Myracles and Second Chances* by facing down some of life's greatest challenges. As you read this book you will become acutely aware that they have been successful because they have believed God for the impossible. In my many years in ministry I have rarely witnessed people who have faced so many challenges with so much grace and faith. Through their faith they have received the miraculous over and over again and their stories of pain and triumph are sure to give you a faith lift.

Kris and Brandi have not just received the miraculous, they have learned the lesson that most miracles do not occur as soon as they are requested or needed. Miracles often occur on the second, third, fourth or even more attempts at trying to reach a successful conclusion. Very few first tries are successful and most of us find ourselves needing a do-over! No worries! The God we serve is a God of second, third and fourth chances!

Think of this, if the Word of God commands us to forgive four hundred and ninety times in a day, how many chances do you think God will give us in the challenges we face?

Buckle your seatbelt and get ready to be encouraged and challenged to continue believing God for what you have need of, as you read *Myracles and Second Chances.*

—*Don Nordin*
Lead Pastor, CT Church
Houston, Texas
myct.church

INTRODUCTION

There was once a little boy who was a little over two years old, but unlike other two year olds, he wasn't meeting his milestones. Not only was he not meeting milestones, he was experiencing extreme difficulty with his development, his communication and his behavior. "They" said he would never be able to achieve the things little boys are supposed to do.

As a parent, I was devastated, shaken to the very core of my being. As a father, I was disappointed, angry, bitter and consumed with guilt. But despite what "they" had said, I never saw him in any way other than my perfect son. I never thought of him in anyway other than being someone who would be spectacular when he grew up. He was a beautiful little one with big hazel eyes and sandy blonde hair. And he was smart, just not in the ways he was supposed to be at that age; he was smart in ways that weren't "tested."

In spite of having a core belief that God always has a plan, during this life-altering trial, I couldn't see it, and even if I did, I probably had a skewed view. I would have never realized what or who this little boy would or could become and I sure didn't know that God had a special plan for my life as a subtitle to his, but I always knew God had a plan for us both.

Looking at him now, you would never guess that the doctors said he would never speak and would most likely have to be put in an institution by the time he was twelve. As a father hearing those words about my child was almost unbearable. I can't express appreciation enough for the village I had around me even then; the friends and family who supported me, held me up and refused to let me give up and quit. The young man many of you know and others of you may know well: His name is Will and he is my son.

Will was the inspiration for our first book, *We Win: A Father's Journey through Autism.* And just as I suspected from the very beginning, Will did have a purpose and one that we could have never imagined. In our second book, Will continues to inspire, encourage and amaze us. As you continue to read, you will see what a great young man he is growing up to be and how, because of a Myracle and a second Chance, he is becoming just who God intended him to be. If you have not read the first book, I suggest you stop and read it first before continuing this one because it will enlighten more of the journey that we all have been asked to walk.

Because of these experiences I am led to ask, "Are you in need of a miracle or possibly a second chance?" Many of you could easily shake your head yes. It might be financial, relational, job related or personal. But despite how perfect your life might seem to others, I don't know anyone who couldn't use a miracle, and most of us could definitely use a second chance or a do-over in some area of our lives.

As a Christian, I strongly believe in the power of prayer, the power of our words, and the power of God. I believe that with God all things are possible! I believe that God is going to show up and do what he said he would do. I believe in second chances, third chances, fourth chances and one hundred chances if that is what it takes to get it right. To some it may seem like way too many chances to give, but it's been proven to me over and over again that he never runs out of chances for us. We often forget that God works in mysterious ways and that one second to God is like a million. He will show up when we least expect it and most often in the unexpected ways. He may appear in many different forms—a whisper in our ear or a scream from the mountaintops.

As you walk this journey with us you will see we have encountered mountaintops and walked through valleys, but whether we walked, crawled, ran or climbed, we have conquered them all.

Brandi and I have a huge population of people that we work with, talk to and love on within the capacity of our jobs. We become part of their lives and they become part of ours; it is what we call "the village" and without it we wouldn't be able to do what we do to help kids, including our own. Throughout this book, we will be sharing some follow up stories of our village that you met in book one. You will also be introduced to new members in our village whom we hope you fall in love with just like we have. Our hope is that you will laugh some, cry more and have a few "ah ha" moments along the way, but that in the end you will see a reflection of him.

As you walk alongside us as you read and feel the stares and glares, joys and sorrows, and the trials and triumphs, keep in mind that just like us, you, too, can find yourself right smack dab in the middle of a miracle or blessed enough to be given a second chance. Also keep in mind that, sometimes instead of receiving, we can be a miracle for someone else or provide that much needed second chance. Love, grace, mercy and kindness can go a long way. Despite color, social standings or financial success, we all have battles to face, and until we have walked in someone else's shoes, we do not know or fully understand the hardships or trials they may face on a daily or even moment-to-moment basis.

This thing known as life throws obstacles of all kinds to us all. But for those of us who will endure, in due season we will see a miracle and/or a second chance or maybe even more! We have all been blessed to cross paths with one another for some reason, season or a specific time and place.

It is no accident or coincidence that you read book one and are reading this now. Welcome. It automatically makes you a member of our village. However, we need participants in this journey, not spectators. Are you in? Where are you in your journey? Do you find yourself in the midst of trials or immense struggle and heartache, or are you on the mountaintop, experiencing contentment? What are you in need of? Have you found your "why"? What about your purpose? Our wish as you read this book is that from our experiences, you will find the motivation to be the hands and feet of Jesus because at the end of the day that is all that matters.

1
UPDATE ON
THE JOURNEY

Wow, what a ride this has become since we last left you in *We Win: A Fathers Journey through Autism* several years ago. If you have not had a chance to read the first book I suggest you do so before continuing on with this one. These updates will be a lot more meaningful and will make more sense to you. If not, then sit back, relax and enjoy the ride with us!

Will's accomplishments have only continued since we last left you. He has blossomed into a great young man who is well liked by his peers and adults, too.

Special Olympics has been a vital part of our lives since Will was old enough to participate. It is a wonderful organization that has allowed him to partake in events like track and field, basketball, and now swimming that he otherwise would not have gotten to enjoy!

Special Olympics hosts a state competition with a variety of events for which one must qualify to become eligible for in order to compete in late May. Swimming has always been one of his favorite things about summer. He loves the water and, because drowning is such a threat to individuals on the spectrum, he took swimming lessons when he was very young. So why not turn something into a competition to help nurture those important life skills that we have taught him from an early age?

Will's qualifying for state in swimming was the highlight of our year! To parents of special needs children, it is like our Super Bowl, the playoffs or the National Spelling Bee. The experience is like no other, the air is filled with excitement, pride and amazement as you watch people of all ages and capabilities compete for their chance to be the gold, bronze or silver medalist in their preferred sport. Watching Will win a gold and silver medal in his events at his first swimming competition was nothing short of miraculous. He loved the attention, was smiling from ear to ear and waving as if he were a Olympic star.

And although I had reservations and had to fight the nervousness, worries and "what ifs" that made their way into my mind, Will continues to teach me that we can never say someone can't do something; we just may need to say they can't do it yet!

Years ago, I resigned myself to the fact that he would probably not be an honor graduate, go to college or be an academic scholar. I see now that it was wrong of me to have thought that way, though honestly, at times that is how I think. But in true Will fashion, I received a phone call from the counselors office requesting our presence at the awards ceremony at Will's school.

In the past he had received awards—the character award, student of the month and perfect attendance. (For those who teach special education, you know we don't keep our kids home unless we have to.) Assuming this award would be something of the same, only one of us was going to miss work to attend—until we received a call from the teacher and his principal asking that we both come. Our curiosity was peaked as to why our attendance was so valuable. It was a huge request, not because of our inability to attend, or our lack of wanting to.

Will easily becomes anxious when both parents are together at one of his functions, especially if it is somewhere we are not normally together, such as his school. He has difficulty understanding why we are there, assumes something is wrong, and finds it difficult to assess the situation and know what rules apply and who is in charge.

If you have a child with special needs then you probably didn't need that explanation, but for those that don't, hopefully this explains why you sometimes might see parents lurking in the dark corners at your kids' school.

After much debate and weighing the pros and cons, we decided to give it a try. Worst case scenario: one of us would have to leave. Best case: We would both be there to share in the receipt of this award, whatever it was. We both attended the assembly hoping for the best outcome and it surpassed our wildest dreams. After watching the many other students called out and congratulated for their academic success, we grew hopeful of what was in store for Will.

Much to our amazement, Will received the English Award for the year. Now as awesome as this is, you can't imagine the pride we felt considering this is the same individual that they told me would never speak just a few years back; the same young man, they said would have to be put in an institution by the time he was twelve. I sat there utterly speechless. My son had just received an award in English because he had made such an improvement speaking and communicating. To say I felt validated doesn't even come close. I wanted to shout it to the world that those who had made those statements against him all the times before were wrong. I am sure I had tears of joy running down my face as I realized how much progress he had made and was continuing to make.

As I sat there in sheer unbelief, I heard his name called out again. Will had made the A/B Honor Roll. What? Am I hearing things? I could hardly contain myself as I watched him walk up and accept this award for the hard work he had done that a sense of accomplishment and again like he was a superstar. I was amazed. I was honored. I was humbled. My child, whom the world often sees as inept, damaged, or "less than," had risen above his circumstances with the help of others to make something out of nothing.

Will is my true hero and the best teacher I have ever had in my life! I have a hard time saying "I can't" anymore because I see what he goes through on a daily basis, usually with a smile. I admire him so much. He has helped me and others more than he will ever know. He gives hope and encouragement to so many on this journey. To know him is to love him. I love him big—and bigger by the day it seems.

One of Will's big passions in life is VHS tapes. He loves VHS tapes, so much that he has thousands of them. He has never been a big fan of DVDs or even TV shows for that matter. His love for VHS tapes is mainly due to the fact that he can fast

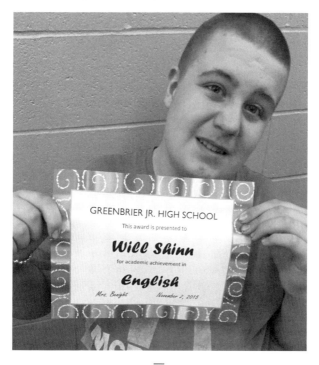

forward a movie, rewind to the very spot that is his favorite and hit rewind a million times, so much so we have a stack of VCRs in his closet because they have to be replaced so often.

As surprising as it may seem, Will transitioned possibly better than any of us with the arrival of Myracle and Chance. It has been amazing to watch the progress and accomplishments that have occurred since their arrival.   Based on all we know about autism, the change in our family structure could have been disastrous, but as we have mentioned time and time again, God had a plan and in his infinite wisdom. He knew all Will Shinn needed was a Myracle and a Chance!

As the pictures reflect, he has taken well to his new role as 'big bubba' in addition to all the other roles he plays in his world. He can often be seen carrying diaper bags, pushing the stroller, bringing us diapers, holding bottles and even sharing his iPad to watch videos.

He has also been known to get them out of their baby beds when they are crying, taking them a bottle or picking up the toy they have dropped for the hundredth time.

As with any big brother, he is fiercely protective. One of the most surprising things I've witnessed has been Will's response to strangers who approach the twins. He often gets between the person and the twins, basically getting "all up in their business" until he figures out that they are okay or receives the stand down from us. Considering that one of the main characteristics for a child with autism, especially one who is viewed as moderate to severe, is a lack of development in relationships, this is a very big deal. But make no mistake, Will is very protective of his little ones, that you can be sure of!

When Myracle and Chance joined our family and started watching cartoons on the television, guess who joined in? Yes, he sat on the floor with a swing or bouncy seat on either side of him, laughing and cooing right along with them. As they have gotten older and have shown an interest in what he is doing, he has also begun to share his iPad, which continually blows us away. It has been spellbinding to watch how these three—who cannot speak—communicate with each other in their own ways. To say they share a special bond would require light years of explaining.

As you read in the first book, *We Win: A Father's Journey through Autism*, we were told Will would never speak. But just like all other aspects of his life, where there is a will there is a way. As the twins have reached milestones, Will has joined them. His speech has picked up steam and his vocabulary has increased drastically. I suppose having two little ones on the same verbal level with him has been more effective than adults teaching him to babble and coo. With each new day we continue to hear more words and so much more social interaction! It is an amazing journey!

Due to his new found self-confidence and his coveted role of big brother, Will now orders most of his own food at restaurants, granted they have also learned how to understand him. It often takes us by surprise when people who haven't seen him in some time tell us how much he has advanced. The progress is undeniable.

God is good all the time and all the time God is so, so good! Truly the best is yet to come, but we are living some of those years of hard work, sweat and tears. At times I find myself sitting with tears streaming thinking about where we were and where we could have easily been if not for God. I am incredibly thankful for where we are today. I am truly a blessed man in so many ways. It reminds me of the old song, "Had It Not Been." God truly has ordered my steps, even though I challenged his plan several times, I am sure. He has never given up on me, but carried me when I couldn't walk and gave me the strength when I couldn't make it on my own.

Stay in the race, keep on going and lean on him. Continue to have hope because he will never give up on you.

—

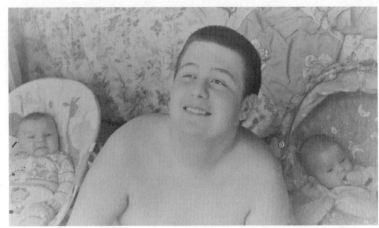

2
A MYRACLE
& A CHANCE

*Miracle: "An extraordinary event manifesting
divine intervention in human affairs."
Chance: "Something that happens unpredictably
without discernible human intention or observable cause."
—Webster's Dictionary*

I have always heard you should never ask for things unless you are certain you want to receive them. Because as life would have it, sometimes you get exactly what you asked for, and other times you get double.

Brandi and I were raised believing that with God all things were possible. We also learned from experience that God's timing is perfect and sometimes we have to walk the walk of faith believing in things that aren't seen. Some of life's greatest testimonies have come from walking through trials of great faith, and ours is no exception. We want to share these with you in hopes that you would continue to believe or strengthen your own faith and keep looking for your own miracle and chance!

It is amazing to look back now and see how God was orchestrating every intricate detail of this story. It was part of his plan—the trials, hardships, and the pain along the way. He was giving us our own "Myracle" and second "Chance." Throughout her life, Brandi fought endometriosis, polycystic ovarian disease (even having an ovary removed at the young age of fourteen for precancerous cells) and was diagnosed with adenomyosis, which is very unheard of in someone so young. And for those like me who have no idea what any of these foreign names mean, each pertains to female reproductive issues.

When I met Brandi she was in remission. Our meeting was an answer to prayer for both of us, but to Brandi it was also what she believed was God's divine way of fulfilling a promise he had made her. With the guidance of her doctor, Brandi had taken part in every experimental technique, drug and surgery in an effort to preserve her one remaining ovary. She was willing to save this organ at all cost. To her it was the family "jewel" and, at this point in time, it was functioning.

Our meeting is a testimony in itself, what some would even refer to as divine or miraculous. We knew on our first

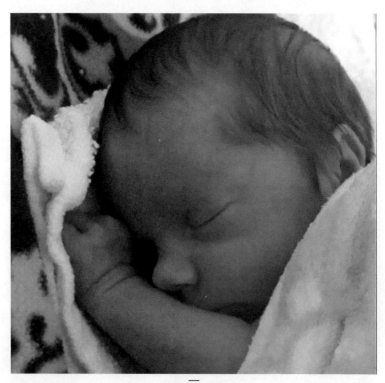

date we would marry. We were engaged within two months and married in ten. Our union created an instant family of five, but her urgency to have a child of her own was still at the forefront of her thoughts. As we built our life together, Brandi easily adjusted into the job she had always longed for, that of being a mother, even if it was only part time. She loved my kids from my first marriage whom she quickly referred to as hers, too. Yet she still longed to have the title of "mom."

Despite our best efforts, becoming pregnant never happened. As the years passed, Brandi's disappointment and concern begin to grow, but she continued to stand on the promise that she would be a mother—not just a "bonus mom" to the children who shared our home on weekends and holidays, but a full-time mom. Her doctor was in full agreement. You can only imagine the heartache she felt realizing that, despite her continued belief that God would stand by his promise and her intriguing thought that she would be a modern day version of Abraham's wife, Sarah, a total hysterectomy was her only choice. Brandi documented her feelings during this time on her blog.

When surgery was first mentioned, I wanted to wait...I had fought these demons before and wasn't willing to give up so easily. When you have held on to hope for thirty years that one day you will have a baby, it's not something to let go of easily.

I used my work as the perfect excuse. My husband and I own an autism and behavioral consulting business. We have many clients and school districts that I couldn't just leave hanging during the middle of the school year.

The doctors seemed to understand my point, and were willing to wait until I couldn't handle the pain anymore. But what they didn't see was that my real thoughts were less about work and clients and more about knowing this was my last chance. I was trying to buy some extra time for God—he has one last shot to come through for me. I had prayed, believed, hoped, cried, stood on scriptures and even reminded God what a great mom I would be. Even bargaining with him. But it apparently didn't matter.

We are three days away and I am not pregnant. It looks like the end is in sight. Something I have dreamed about since childhood is not going to happen. I couldn't wait to be pregnant, to start our little family. I had a plan as to how to tell my hubby the news and our families. And it would have been spectacular. But again, it doesn't look like it's going to happen. And, yes, I am mad! Mad because I adore kids! Mad 'cause I like kids better than most adults. Mad because God didn't see me fit enough to allow me to have even just one? I would take a house full. But no! Why? What's so bad about me? I feel like if I really knew why, it might make it better.

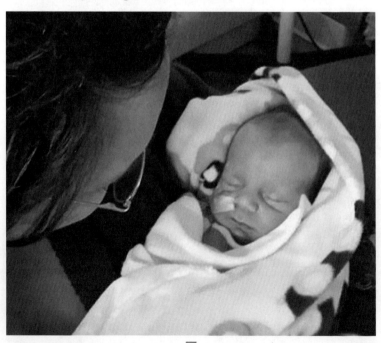

Then there is the bitterness—or resentment—that settles in towards those who have babies they don't want or don't take care of. Yet they still keep having them. Or what about the ones who leave them in the car seat for five days without food, water or diaper change? How do they deserve a baby?

I then become overwhelmed by the deep-seated issues of womanhood. I am having a total hysterectomy. They are removing every organ that identifies and entitles me as a woman. So after Monday when all female parts are gone, do I officially become a nobody? Not real sure how I feel about that.

I already feel guilty for not being able to give my husband a child by me. One that is a perfect mixture of us. A little girl I had imagined and dreamed about for years. With dark curly hair like her mama and big blue eyes like her daddy and a smile that lights up a room. Just another dream that is crashing down around me. And then the guilt associated with wanting my own baby when I have Will. He is the light of my life, but he has nothing of mine. No, it doesn't matter to me in terms of loving him. It bothers me in terms that he isn't really mine and in the back of my head I think someone will take him away from me one day.

It seems my hopes and dreams are dying off (being cut out one by one). How does one handle that? What emotions am I supposed to feel?

My heart aches for a tiny piece of me that I will never have. My heart longs for the heartbeat of the soul I created. My arms ache from the loneliness.

Although I have stepchildren I adore and love as my own, I have wanted Kris and I to have one together. And in some ways because of Will, we do. But it's just not the same.

My prayer for Monday is that God will provide me

with the peace I need to get through the surgery and the feelings that come with it. I then pray he will begin to fill that void and that loss with something that brings me much joy!

I do not want to dwell on the past. I want to move forward with my family. But until then, "Bye bye, baby, bye bye." I'm sorry I never knew you. If I had, you would've had a great mama and daddy who would have loved and adored you.

This news, as you can imagine, was a tremendous blow to both of us. Brandi was distraught and puzzled as to how God was going to fulfill a promise she knew he had made her during her teen years. I mean God is God, I know, but it would be pretty miraculous when you don't have the parts, right?

And though we laughed about her thoughts of being a modern day version of Sarah, I can't help but be reminded of another great promise, the promise that God gave to Abraham and Sarah. I can only imagine they possibly felt the same way we were feeling. How in the world was she going to have a baby at the ripe ole age of old? I can't help but also be reminded of the greatest story ever told, the birth of our Christ. How could a virgin conceive a child and how would Joseph handle all of that?

God did the miraculous in Bible days, right? He often fulfilled promises and did the unusual. We have heard these stories for years. But how would God bring this about in our lives in the modern day without us turning into the next show on the circus. That was our question, too, and yet, she still believed.

The surgery was a success, if that is what you call it. Thankfully her recovery was less than normal due to a new robotic surgery. Despite her belief that God was able, Brandi remained unsettled that year. She had great difficulty accepting the end of her "womanhood" (as she referred to it) as well as the death of a dream. She couldn't see or understand "why." It was a very tough time for me, too, because I knew the desire of her heart and had no idea how to make that happen. Truth be told, I could not make it happen all along because it was always in God's hands. All of life is.

Fast forward ten months. On December 16, 2014, in Benton, Arkansas, a set of twins was born, a little girl and a little boy. Born early and in an emergency situation. They were taken via C Section due to a placenta abruption. The two little ones were given the names Myracle and Chance. They were my niece and nephew, my wife's sister's children.

Despite her grief at the missed opportunity at motherhood and surgery months before, Brandi visited them often during their stay at the NICU. The twins were born premature and needed continual care. I never visited them, and now I really wished I had.

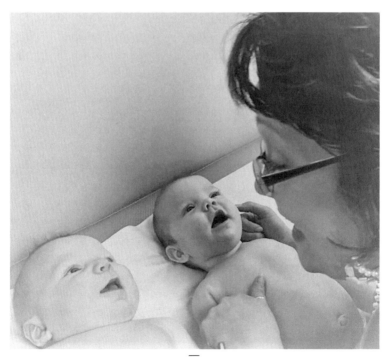

3
AND THEN THERE WERE SEVEN

As I take a deep breath and shake my head, it seems surreal that there are seven of us, yes, seven! I had never thought of myself as having a large family. Brandi came from a large family and wanted nothing more, but I had grown up in a family of four and had felt super blessed having my family of five.

And yet, here we were at seven, the number of completion. In Genesis the number seven is identified with something being "finished" or "complete." Through scripture after scripture this association continues as seven is found in contexts involving completeness or divine perfection. In Exodus 22:30 the command is given that the animals are to be at least seven days old before being used for sacrifice. The leper Naaman was told to bathe in the Jordan River seven times in order to be cleansed (2 Kings 5:10). And how many times was Joshua commanded to march around Jericho? You got it, seven times! In just these few instances the number seven signifies a completion, orchestrating a divine mandate fulfillment.

Here's how our story of seven began.

Me: "Hello, Honey, I am in the middle of class!"

Brandi: "I know, but I really need to talk to you right now!"
Me: "Okay, give me just a second and I will call you back."

I questioned what could be so urgent that Brandi would call me when she knew I had class, and it had me more than a little worried.

I immediately announced to the class: "I need to take a break for a few minutes and call my wife back. Obviously there are some issues going on at home and I need to find out what she needs and what I need to do. We will resume class in a few minutes."

Praying everyone was okay, I made the call.

"Honey, what is up? Is something wrong with Will? Are you okay? What has happened?"

Questions were flooding my mind and I couldn't get them out as fast as I was thinking them.

"Will is fine, but no, Kris, we have a different issue," Brandi said.

With just her response of "Kris," I knew something was up. Since we had met, my wife had seldom called me Kris, most often it was terms of endearment like "Honey" and especially on the phone. So the red flags of this conversation were flying high.

I buckled up, preparing myself for the worst in hopes that she was overreacting. (Those who know her well know she does that often.) Or perhaps I was over analyzing. (Those who know me, know that's a great possibility as well.) Our conversation continued.

Brandi: "You remember we were supposed to keep the twins this weekend right?" (My niece and nephew, who at the time were only three months old.)
Me: "Yes, I remember."
Brandi: "Well, I am on my way to get them because they are going to need to stay with us for a few days."

This was on a Monday, the first day of a training class that lasted four days out of town. My first thought was there was no way we can do this. We work!

Brandi was supposed to be at work even then. Neither of us were young enough to handle a newborn day and night for a couple of days, much less premature twins. My thoughts then quickly shifted to Will. And what about Will? How is a fourteen-year old with severe autism not going to be disrupted from his daily life? This will rock his world!

The scenarios, excuses, and millions of reasons why this was not a good idea fluttered around in my head as my mind came back to the conversation, but knowing Brandi like I did, I knew she had her mind made up before she called. This was merely a courtesy call letting me know of her decision.

Me: "Okay, Honey, if that is what you want to do. But you will have to do it alone because I am out of town."

Brandi: "Kris (again using my first name, confirming in my mind that she was doing it regardless of what I said or did not say), I am not sure we have a choice. I am going to get them and we will just have to do our best."

As I walked back into class, the weight of our conversation settled in, so much so that apparently I had a look of despair

on my face. The attendees in my training class begin throwing questions at me like a dart board.

"Is everything ok?" "What happened?" "What can we do to help?"

Taking another big breath, I explained what had occurred and how it appeared my family's little world was changing significantly for "a couple of days," as stated by my wife. I looked out at them for encouragement, motivation and help, but saw eyes of shock and concern staring back at me.

The day proceeded and I did my best not to become too consumed with what was going on elsewhere. Fortunately for me, I had a class full of women who did their best to assure me that things were going to be okay.

During the week, I had very little contact with Brandi. I knew she undoubtedly had her hands full. When Friday finally arrived and I returned home, she looked as though she had been through the wringer cycle on the washing machine indefinitely, and yet despite the sleepless nights, and the extreme adjustments, she had a smile on her face like none I had ever witnessed before.

As she began to tell me the details of her week, I was

impressed with her efforts, resilience and sheer grit, yet mystified by the fact that we had two tiny humans living in our house staring back at me. I had not been around a baby for several years and had for sure never had two the same age at the same time and so very little.

Brandi, knowing me like she does, immediately began to see overwhelming apprehension sweeping across my face like a flashing neon sign. Immediately she began conjuring up words of affirmation and assurance.

"It is only going to be for about fifteen days or so. We can do anything for fifteen days. We can do this, Kris, and if you can't do it, then please just do it for me."

And just like that our journey as a family of seven had begun.

4
YOU MIGHT
AS WELL JUMP

Do you ever have the sinking feeling that your day isn't
going to work out quite like you planned, even before you've
had that first cup of coffee? Days you want to go back to bed,
pull the covers over your head and hide? Weeks when you feel
the black cloud over your head just won't go away? Times that
life is so overwhelming it seems impossible things could get any
worse, and you begin to think, "I just cannot do this anymore"?

We have all had those days, I can assure you. I too have had
many of those days. But through those days I have learned that
despite it all, there is hope. There is always hope, no matter how
bleak our situation may appear, hope no matter what others
may say, and hope, no matter how we might feel.

I want to challenge you to jump. Yes, you "might as well
jump!"

Don't panic, I am not encouraging you to jump off the
nearest bridge, or drive your car off a cliff, although sometimes
in our darkest moments some of us may have entertained
the idea for a split second. What I am asking you to do is to
embrace the idea of taking that leap of faith. Think back. Are

—
39

there times in your life you missed great opportunities because you weren't willing to take a chance? Make the jump *per se*. This is not a recommendation to be foolish; this is merely a proposition for you to consider. We all reach a point in our lives that if we want to make a difference within ourselves, children, marriage, job, community and world, we must take a leap of faith to do what it is we were placed in this world to do.

In early 2012, Brandi had come to a crossroad in her business. She was receiving requests for services that we couldn't offer due to lack of personnel. She began discussing with me the need to offer crisis management classes in the schools she was serving. Through various discussions we had made the determination her schedule didn't allow the time needed to get trained and teach the classes. On what I thought was a whim, she begin suggesting that I get trained and provide the class, claiming I would be perfect due to my athletic ability and the simple fact that I was a male in a predominately female profession.

I thought she was nuts! I laughed, reminding her I was not qualified in the slightest way. She continued to persuade me with what I considered "buttering me up" with the notion I had a story to tell, and what better person to do it than the father of a son with autism who stood to benefit from these services.

Adamantly, I continued to disagree; surely she had lost her mind. I found it difficult even talking to family and close friends about Will and his disability and yet she wanted me to talk to complete strangers. I continued to dismiss her crazy yet passionate pleas and moved on with my sales career. It was where I felt comfortable, where I found success and where my experience was. I had been in sales for close to twenty years with a Business Administration degree. Why on earth would I want to change careers, especially to a totally different field?

Much to my dismay, she did not give up easily. She continued to bring up the subject occasionally, making sure she wasn't pushing too hard to the point of complete and total defiance on my part. She knew well enough that if I was backed into a corner, she would never be able to win me over to her cause.

A couple of months passed and she approached me with the subject again, and this time she would not relent. As I had before, I declined. I didn't have the expertise or the ability to do what she was asking, much less with professional educators. Ignoring my claims, she asked me to research some prominent systems and share my opinions. As I began my search, I became keenly aware that maybe she was on to something. I marched on with my research, sent emails and made phones calls to the systems I found to be the most intriguing.

After weeks of talking with others, looking at data, considering the needs of my own child, listening to my heart, my mind and spirit, I gave her the answer I felt was best for students, parents, and educators. The one I felt would be best for her to pursue for the business.

I was in total agreement at this point that crisis management training was something her business needed to offer, although I still didn't feel any more convinced I was the one who should teach it. She would not let it go. She stood by her belief that I was the one to do it for the business.

Reluctantly I agreed to pray about it some more, with total confidence her idea of me being involved was as crazy as before. Much to my surprise after a lot of praying, soul searching and questioning God's plan, I felt teaching crisis management training was, indeed, what I needed to do.

I prepared my resignation letter and in October I resigned my sales job to join my wife's business full time. To say that was a total leap of faith is an understatement. I was leaving my full-time job to go to work with my wife with no real idea of what I was doing. I had no idea if we would be able to replace my income and, if so, how long it would take. I spent the better part of that weekend forming a plan. My plan of how things should go, when they should go, and where.

At that point in my life, I hadn't really learned how to follow the voice of God into the areas of the unknown. I was all about following God's calling when everything was laid out or fit into the confines of my plan. Following God's calling into unfamiliar territory outside of my comfort zone was something new and very uncomfortable, but God would quickly teach me.

Within three days of my resignation, I received a phone call from a former co-worker who needed my help. I was able to replace my full-time income with a very part-time second job. Two months later, I attended class to become a crisis management certified trainer in schools, facilities, and other settings. We had no idea how or if this would work, but we would make our way through it. It was almost three months later before I would teach my first class.

In just a few short years of teaching this system, we found we needed additional help in order to train all the people who wanted to be trained. I was working more than I had ever dreamed and my job description had grown to include consulting within the schools. I can't help but be thankful for my wife's constant prodding and persistence. Despite my continued resistance she never gave up. God had given her a glimpse into the future of a business that included me.

I am thankful that I entertained her thoughts eventually, researched and then spent time in prayer reflecting on what God perhaps wanted for my life instead of what I thought was most comfortable. Making that jump was the best thing I could have done. Finding my "why" or "purpose" in this thing we call life has been most rewarding.

Although some jumps we take are bigger than others, all leaps of faith can be life changing. Writing my first book was also another leap out of my comfort zone. It is very scary to display one's raw and most intimate feelings to the world during difficult times. Even more difficult for me is putting those feelings and events into words on a page. Despite having what some would refer to as the "gift of gab" and easily relating to people in person, putting my thoughts in writing is much more difficult. I really want to convey my feelings in such a way that you, the reader, experience it right along with me.

Probably one of the biggest jumps I, along with my family, have taken was the addition of the twins to our family. As a couple in our forties with three teenagers, one of whom is disabled, taking in newborns was definitely a huge jump. As with other jumps, this one was more than out of our comfort zone. By all accounts, we were too old to have been getting newborns, much less two of them. But it's the jumps we take that often make our lives complete.

I think God chuckles when we plan our lives without consulting him. You would think we would have all learned by now that our plans are most often not cohesive with his in the end. Our plans may not be bad or wrong, but they sure aren't as blessed as they could be if we followed his more than ours. "Might as well jump" sums up life when you put all of your trust in the One who knows. We are often too comfortable where we are or too scared to change, but sometimes it takes us making the jump. Following the leading of others, slowing down, and listening.

The title of this chapter is not just an empty saying. "Might as Well Jump" is a way of life. It is a call to better ourselves and trust in the One who created us. We have been led to where we are today through a series of events and things in our lives which prepared us for this moment. Let's not miss feeling the fresh breeze on our faces as we make the jump. Let's take a leap of faith, find our purpose, make a difference, and seek God's finest for our lives.

The biggest regrets I have in life are those opportunities I missed. Opportunities I missed because I refused to jump but instead chose to stay in my comfort zone or in the safety of my own four walls. The gauntlet has been cast and the time to jump is at hand. Jump into your purpose, jump into your "why," and into the new day that awaits you. You can do it and you will not regret it!

Will you take the chance? Will you rise above it all to reach new heights and destinations?

Jump!

5
EVEN THOUGH I WALK

I want to share a little more insight into me—Kris, the person. Some of what I am sharing is probably relatable. You may have been there too, possibly, or know someone close to you who has. Or you can grasp it from your experiences and point of view. For others, this may be beyond what you have ever imagined or even thought about at any given time.

My purpose is to invite you to step into our world. The miracles we experienced were often brought to light after tumultuous times. In saying that, please let me assure you that neither Brandi nor I want sympathy; we have faced circumstances just like everyone. It is this thing called life, and in it no one gets a free pass. No one is free of trials, heartaches, sicknesses or strife. What we do want is to shed a light in order for others to be more understanding and accepting of things that don't fit within the norm. The true picture of our understanding and acceptance comes through the help we receive or give. Empathy is a great trait to possess, but an even better one to display. Join with me now as we explore the me that most people never see.

I have been walking this road of autism for many years as a dad, and joined the realms of educator/consultant a few years back. A father to five kids, two of which live with their mom two hours away, the other three in our house. We are constantly on the go.

My job often requires me to travel, sometimes within the state and often out of state. My job description allows me to be in a variety of school districts on a daily basis and in different educational settings within those schools. I have the privilege of meeting and working with some of the finest staff members and families I could ever hope to meet.

Is each day met with some sort of challenge of what I do? Yes, there are many, and just like you, some days are more challenging than others. But one thing that sets Brandi and me apart from many others in our line of work is that not only do we meet extreme obstacles at work, we have them at home, too.

Due to Will's diagnosis of autism, most tasks that would be easy for a teen his age is very difficult or at times impossible for him to conduct without some assistance or supervision. Simple tasks that many have taken for granted since their children became school-aged are complex, such as talking, doing small household chores or bathing. Then with the addition of the twins, our duties became even more engrossed. It is basically like having a man-sized toddler and two infants.

We are often asked, "How on earth do you do this?" or the occasional, "I have no idea how you and Brandi do it, I could never."

To these I reply tongue-in-cheek, "Well, when we figure it out I will tell you, too," or, "I do not know how you don't." With my travels, I am out of town often and I must say, my wife is definitely the glue that holds it all together on most days. She is amazing; even though she will try to convince you she is not. I devoted an entire chapter to her in the first book to her dedication and love for Will, Emma and Kate and our family as a unit. Her dedication and love has not waivered over the years, but has only become stronger with the addition of the twins. The ride has definitely increased in speed and craziness, but she continues to be the lead in my absence. We are blessed.

So how do we do it? When God calls you to it, he will see you through it. That is our motto. That is our mantra and often our saving grace.

Many of the children I see in our line of business are fighting battles that would literally break your heart. They often face social isolation, emotional abandonment, and learning difficulties that kids should never have to face. And yet as adults we often criticize them for their behavior, their lack of attention and skills. But what they need from us is a "Myracle and a Chance," not more condemnation, judgment or ridicule from the adults who were intended to be their role models.

In the opportunities I have to speak with others, I often stress the importance of just being human; how kindness and following the golden rule of "doing unto others as you would have others do unto you (or more importantly, your children or grandchildren)" can make all the difference. As adults we are their peek into the future as to what life will be like when they grow up. In every walk of life, regardless of profession, are remarkable individuals who strive daily to make a difference in the lives of those they come into contact with, but we need more. We need you; more importantly, they need you!

Challenges are numerous and the answers are few, but we must never give up, give in or give out finding them. Our children and world depend on us getting things right more often than wrong. Love can conquer a vast majority of things, but it is hard to pour from an empty glass if you do not have others pouring into you. Thankfully, I am blessed to be surrounded by many who pour into me on a daily basis. Some within the circle I talk to everyday while others it may be only occasional and in text or email form. But you see, I learned a valuable lesson years ago to surround myself with people I wanted in my corner because in this world you can only really trust a few and should listen to advice from even less. The people in my circle of confidants are of varying occupations; some of which would surprise you while others most would expect.

One of my confidants has been in my corner since I can remember, actually even before I could remember. My dad. If asked, he would tell you that he just did the best he could with what he knew. He taught me the value of being kind and respectful while challenging the rules and the ones who made them in order to make this world a better place. He taught me to be my best always; never expecting perfection, but instead maximum effort in everything I did.

As a child growing up, I remember report card day, back when they were printed on card stock and folded in two, making it four pages. Not the online version that many of you only know. I would come home sometimes possibly anxious and at other times proud. I would place it in front of him for him to look over. With anticipation I would wait while he peered over the markings, not realizing at the time why he was the most interested in my behavior grade. Being the kind and respectful young boy I was, I always received the "S." Back in the day, you had two options, "S" for satisfactory, which was the best, or "U" for unsatisfactory. Pretty cut and dry I would say.

It was only then he would study my grades in each subject knowing full well what the markings were going to be before I had even brought them home. I enjoyed the luxury, some might say, of having a mother who was a teacher. After his examination was complete, Dad would look at me right in the eye and he always asked the same question regardless of the marks, the grade I was in, or the age I was.

"Kris, is this best you can do?" he would ask.

There were times I could look at him solely in the eyes and with total confidence say "yes." Yet there were more times I could not. His expectation of me and my performance is still a driving force this very day. Although those lessons are long gone, I have never forgotten the impact that had on me. It taught me the lesson that hard work pays off in the long run, that if you work and do your best, you can never be disappointed in your performance. You can be let down because of circumstances often beyond your control, but never let yourself down because you didn't do your best. He instilled in me the knowledge that you never give up just because it looks hopeless. He taught me that with God there is always hope.

Although the years have passed and the report cards have advanced, he continues to ask that same question. I am often at my parents due to my travel schedule, and as you might expect, any time I walk through their door, my dad will ask me, "Did you give it your best today?" Thankfully with age I have gained more wisdom and I, more often than before, can look him square in the eye and with more confidence than I thought possible and say, "Yes!" I gave all I had to give today and more than I knew I ever could.

Sometimes, even though I have been doing this adult thing more years than not, I find myself facing my own struggles, feeling ill equipped to do what I do. I question why anyone, much less educational experts who often have more degrees than sense, would consult with someone like me.

How could I help others when most would think I need help myself? But just like many of the kids I see, I too needed my own Myracle and Chance. Although a college graduate, I do not have an education degree. I am often asked if I consider myself an expert, to which I quickly respond, "There are no experts." There are people who have a vast knowledge of subjects, some have practical experience and some have none. Reality has given me the best platform; but at the end of the day, when God has called you to do his will, the insight, direction and knowledge he provides will allow you to do more than you ever would have been given in any other circumstance.

Not too very long ago a friend sent me an inspirational

—

video that changed my perspective. It was a live demonstration of finding your "why." As I watched I began to feel a change in how I viewed what I do. In this life we all walk a path, some paths we feel obliged to, others we may feel are our destiny, and sometimes we were just hurled and that is where we landed. But how you look at the path you are on sometimes makes all the difference. Your why in life is the very thing that calls you into existence. It is the purpose of your path. You may be on the path you are meant to be on whether accidentally or with intent, but do you do it with the passion of your "why?" Once you know your purpose then there are very few things that can stop you from fulfilling that call.

For years, I felt I was supposed to help people, which lead me to a career in sales, and other reasons like I could not do accounting very well! I always had a purpose behind what I did to help people and the fact that I made a good living for my family didn't hurt either. Yet, I always felt like there was a void, an empty space that never was quite filled. Longing to fill the void and stay within the realm I was most comfortable, I ventured into other sales positions: beverage equipment, sporting goods, industrial electronics and medical. And still yet, something was missing. One day out of the blue, Brandi says, "I think you need to go to work with me." Feeling dissatisfied with everything I had tried thus far, I decided to take the leap. I felt in my spirit it could be what I had been searching for. We both had a peace about the change and I was officially going to work at Above All Else Inc.

The story from the Bible about Peter walking on water comes to mind. "If you are ever going to walk on the water, you must first step out of the boat." I decided to step out of that boat in late 2012, unsure if I would walk or drown us all. I am proud to say it was one of the best decisions I have ever made; of course, Brandi would say it is because I listened to her. Regardless of all the reasons, it was a huge leap of faith. Above All Else, Inc. had been in business for some time with

Brandi as the sole employee, and although her financial gains assisted our family, it was not our primary source of income. With this leap of faith, we had to rely solely on our business to support the family. As the role of husband and father, it is my main responsibility to make sure we can take care of our family; nevertheless, I knew it was the right thing to do and had a peace that couldn't be explained. The first year was touch and go at times, I am sure we had our moments of weakness where we thought, "What have we done?" yet we remained focused on the task at hand, helping people. Although this journey has had many ups, downs and entirely too many loops, one thing remains constant. It is our purpose and now we know it is our "why."

When I started with the business full time in 2012, Will was doing well. We rocked along for several years. The business was holding its own and we were both doing what we loved. With the arrival of the twins, the business pretty much solely rested on me. Brandi was adapting to motherhood, taking care of

two newborns and Will on the home front. She had trained me well, and the addition of life experiences I had gained through walking through the fire with Will and his autism had prepared me to take on the role. Looking back now I can see how God was preparing me the entire time. Our business has continued to grow exponentially despite our often mistakes and failures. I feel honored he has allowed me to be in the position to help countless numbers of people in this journey of life.

Owning your own business and watching it grow is very rewarding, but it also includes many nights away from my family and driving thousands of miles. Brandi had laid a great foundation for our business which made it easy to continue the work she had started while she continues to do an amazing job at home raising our tribe. We have our ups and downs, too, but the fact remains that lives are being changed and touched every single day because we let God guide and direct us in every step.

I always want to be the guy that gives credit where it is due and I owe all I do to God. So if you have been one of those who has asked, "How do you do what you do?" now you know my secret. I get up each day and put my pants on one leg at a time just like you do. I do what my dad instilled in me all those years ago and maximize my effort by doing my best and try to leave it better than I found it every day.

Do you want to get better? Do you want to make a difference? Do you feel you are giving it all you have? Do you need a Myracle? Do you need a Chance? Well, today you decide what you do with it. What is your "why"? Do you have a purpose? Yes, each one of us has a purpose in this life. I challenge you to look in that mirror every day and tell that person, "Today you have to get better." You are the only one that can do that. You control it along with God's help to make it better today and fulfill your purpose!

EVEN THOUGH I WALK

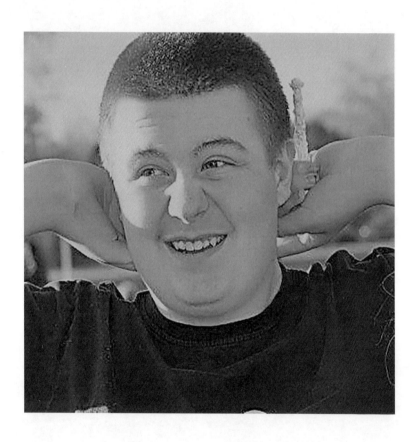

6
COMMON MISTAKES

Mistakes. We've all made them. Some go unnoticed, some are small, while others are life altering. Have you ever made a mistake? Have you ever kept making the same mistake? I know I have. I have made plenty in my lifetime and in some situations I have made the same one for years! Although I strive to be wise and do the right thing, I am human. Sometimes I let my emotions get the best of me and not-so-good decisions are a result. Sometimes we don't realize that the decisions we've made are mistakes until years later.

Mistakes can make you or break you. It is all in how we handle them. Did you learn anything from it, or did you chalk it up as someone else's fault or blow it off as if you don't care?

Within the realm of education and the lives of children, mistakes are made every day. Sometimes they are small ones that come about by accident, others are due to a lack of knowledge and are purely unintentional. Still others occur because adults didn't keep themselves in check and their behavior affected those around them.

Within our profession, we have the opportunity to talk with

teachers nationwide. One common denominator we have found is that most teachers feel very frustrated and overwhelmed by decisions that are not in the best interest of students being made by their government officials and school administrations.

It is difficult for teachers to be in their classrooms required to teach and test concepts over which they have no say and do not feel are appropriate for a child's age or developmental ability. In many cases those decisions cause despondency in our educational providers. Within the professional arena and as parents of a child with a severe disability, we see on a daily basis

how miscommunication, uncontrolled emotions, and a lack of understanding and compassion contribute to mistakes that can be life altering for all involved. Albeit, we can't control what the powers that be do; our focus and goal is to educate teachers, encourage students, and to create more suitable environments so all students can benefit and find success.

As mentioned, mistakes are two-fold. Although always viewed as a negative action, there can be a positive light shown upon them when viewed and treated in the right way. Brandi and I strive to walk what we talk daily. Those of you who know us personally know that "what you see is what you get." We are real. We make mistakes, lots of them. Please know that with each mistake I've listed below is something we have experienced personally. We are not judging or criticizing. We are learning from our mistakes and sharing what we have learned in the hope it will help others. Isn't that what they say about mistakes—that we should learn from them? Mistakes are not always bad. Sometimes they just may not be right for the situation.

Here is a compiled list of what we believe are the most common mistakes we make. Our hope is that by addressing this list, it will cause us to think differently and be more aware than we typically would.

1. *Raising our voice*

Children today have an immense amount of pressure put on them educationally and socially. This often can lead to high amounts of anxiety. When an adult yells, it causes students to go over the top emotionally, sending their anxiety through the roof. They either retreat within themselves and shut down or become combative, neither of which is productive in the home, classroom or community. Keeping our emotions in check, even if that means walking away momentarily, will allow us to speak to children in a calm and relaxed voice. It is the best way to get the most productive results especially if the child is upset.

2. *Not leading by example*

As figures of authority in our homes, educational settings or workplace, if we are not willing to do what we expect those around us to do, we will not get the respect needed to lead. Our children learn by our examples, and if we model the behaviors and characteristics we desire, they will be more likely to conform to our expectations. When we are better, they get better because we expect better. Do for yourself what you expect from others. Our children our living, breathing examples of what we have put before them.

3. *Inconsistency*

The one thing all kids need is consistency. If you tell a child

you are going to do something, then do it. If it is not possible because of unforeseen circumstances, then be honest. Be upfront and tell them you were unable to do what you had said. If possible also tell them the reason you were not able to follow through. Do not ignore and act as though you never told them, hoping they may have forgotten. I promise they do not forget. We work with so many children who believe adults are untrustworthy. They have been told and promised things by adults too many times that never came to pass and were never mentioned again. After being disappointed and betrayed enough, a child begins to not believe what he or she is told.

4. *Improper questioning*

As adults we often create problems for ourselves and in some ways "set up" our children/students to fail by questioning things we already know. For example, "Did I see you take that gum?" "Did you just hit your sister?" "Are you copying his answers?" Of course he is. You saw him take the gum, hit his sister, or copy his neighbor's answers. But by questioning "if" he did or didn't do it, we have given him the opportunity to lie as well, creating a secondary issue to deal with. Most kids will immediately deny what they have been accused of. It is our human nature. We have to be smarter.

5. *Being "inhuman"*

Last time I looked at myself in the mirror, I was a human being. We all are. We laugh, we cry, we have successes and failures. It doesn't matter if we are African-American, Asian, American Samoa, Caucasian, green or purple polka dots. The fact remains we all bleed red, we were all created for a purpose, and we are human. None of us had control of where we were born, to whom we were born or the nationality we were born into. People are people regardless of their circumstances, their mistakes, the color of their skin, their capabilities or disability. Be human.

6. *Not being available*

Our lives have become so fast paced we are constantly bombarded with stuff to do, places to go, responsibilities to take care of. Everything has to get done, yet sometimes we overlook the very people we are doing all those things for—our children, our spouse, families, coworkers, students and friends. Availability to others often takes a back seat to action. But if you ask a child what the best thing is about their parent, it most often includes simple activities involving time, not things or places.

At the end of the day it is not about you or me but about others. Be available to those who need you and have been put in your path. They need you. You need them.

7. *Not "going big"*

I have heard it said all my life to "go big or go home" and I believe it's fact. Love big. Give big. Run big. Walk big. Live big. Speak big. Show big.

8. *Not giving maximum effort*

If perfection is required within your life, you need to modify and accommodate your circle. No one is perfect. with one exception. So although we can't attain perfection, we can give maximum effort every day, in every way and in every situation. Does that mean we will always win or succeed? No, unfortunately not. But it does mean that as long as we are giving 100-percent effort, we will be making a difference somewhere for someone. We will have nothing but pride for ourselves and will have absolutely no guilt for not trying hard. We are a big deal! We matter! We deserve our best.

9. *Is it really about the outcome?*

A common saying in recent years has been, "Enjoy the journey." I often wonder if this came about because someone figured out before everyone else that life was getting out of hand. Have we become so fixed on the outcome, the next step, the next phase, that we have lost the enjoyment and the lessons learned in the journey?

Not everyone will have the same outcome, nor do they desire the same outcome. Not everyone strives to be an honor graduate, a college graduate or the next lawyer. Do we allow ourselves and our expectations to accompany all people? Do we allow people to be themselves without judging and bing supportive of them if their level of achievement is not all we think it should be?

Our max efforts are not the same. What is max effort for you in your situation may not be what I would give. I think our forefathers had the idea many years ago as the penned the old gospel song "I Wouldn't Take Nothing for My Journey Now." Your journey is what you make it, it is who you are and why you are who you are. Learn to enjoy the journey not just the outcomes.

10. *Not getting under the desk*

This is a phrase I tend to use often. It is reflective of situations I have been in when working with others. Many students find solace crawling underneath a literal desk at times; it is quiet, put away from the normal hustle and bustle and gives them a chance to regain control of their emotions or behavior.

Figuratively speaking, I use the phrase as a way to get people to understand that sometimes you have to put yourself in someone else's shoes to truly try and understand where they are coming from or what they see. Personally it also represents to me how we all sometimes need to withdraw from the busyness of our lives, take a deep breath, collect our thoughts and regulate are emotions and behavior.

Here are the eight mistakes I see across all age levels, socioeconomic groups, districts and classes.

1. *Talking too much*

Most of us have never talked anyone out of a crisis situation and we never will, but we do find ourselves in over emotional situations often. Limit your talking. Our continuous talking just adds fuel to an already agitated fire.

2. *Not trusting enough*

We have to learn to trust one another, coworkers, teachers, and those in authority. If you have issues with something they are doing or not doing, address it one on one not in front of others, and especially not in front of other students.

3. *Dying on the hill*

I know you have heard this saying before, but don't die on the mountain trying to get to the battle. So often we as adults pick battles that truly are not worth the fight at the end of the day. Keep the end result in mind, not the petty little things throughout the day

4. *Not preparing for the empty nest*

As parents and educators the goal is for our kids to one day walk out the door and have a successful life of their own. As parents and educators, we have been given a great responsibility in this life to impact the younger generation in one way or another. Our priorities must always be for the betterment of our children. Are you adequately preparing them for the future? Are you confident your child can survive without you if something were to happen? We aren't guaranteed tomorrow; we must live each day in preparation of the next.

5. *Not having a plan*

We are a planning society and if you aren't a planner, that's okay, you can hire one. There are wedding planners, birthday party planners, house planners, and retirement planners. But the things we do not plan are often the things that have the greatest planning needs.

Do you have a living will? Are you an organ donor? If you have a child with severe disabilities, do you have a guardianship plan? Don't wait until it is too late. Don't be the person that after the flood comes who wishes they had flood insurance.

6. *Seeing disability but not ability*

Are there things you have found that you are not good at or just can't seem to do? My dad told me as I was preparing for college that I should be in accounting or sales. After the second semester of accounting, I quickly figured out which one I did not need to do! Most of us gravitate towards things that we are interested in or have a passion for. Kids are no different, but how will they know what they like to do or what their passions are if they are not given the opportunity? We would have never known that Will's passion was band if he had not been given the opportunity. While we don't want to over-involve them, we do want to give them well-rounded ideas and experiences in many things.

Never limit a child because you don't think he has the ability, the talent or the skill to do what his heart desires. There are many people who make lots of money at their profession, not because they have the great looks, the grades, or the skill, but because they had a dream and put in the hard work to accomplish that dream. Don't assume or project your thoughts onto others. Many times people assume Will can't understand because he can't speak well and that is not true. Dreams often get you where other things can't.

7. *Doing less than we are able*

We all tend to focus on what people cannot do like in the previous mistake mentioned. If you can work then you should. If you can make dinner then you should. If you can write your own name then you should! But just because someone cannot do something now doesn't mean they never will. Always strive to be a little better each day, to do what you can, when you can and do your best. Be responsible for your own actions and expect others to be the same. We teach by our example best of all.

So are we doing our best? If so, why is the next generation having so many issues?

8. *Failing to lead like an adult*

Be the best you can be every day because we are the example for the next generation. Be kind, be caring, love big, take smart chances, walk on the water, help all around you, be the better person, fight for right, battle the wrong, and be the example you were meant to be. God placed us here with to make this world a much better place for those we leave behind.

Sometimes we cannot control the roads we have been asked to walk or felt we were thrown on. But we can decide with what attitude we choose to walk them with each and every day. I have always said that your feet will speak volumes about where your thoughts and perspectives are, but your mouth can and will lie about what you want others to believe. I love people, probably too much at times. I want to see you smile, I want to see you succeed and I want you to be the best *you* that there has ever been. You have the control to move your thoughts into actions and your actions into results.

I believe in you and the abilities that God has given to you. You must take the mistakes you have made into consideration when moving forward. Do not look back and relive those moments or let them creep back on you, only use them as stepping stones to your destiny. Do not let others cause you to waiver on your road. Making mistakes is part of life but living in them is not.

Walk on!

7
MEET THEM WHERE THEY ARE

Many years ago I sat in a psychologist's office in Batesville, Arkansas, where my son attended a developmental preschool. I was lost as dad, husband and person. I had not seen the progress I was looking for in Will. I was beyond frustrated, not only with the situation, but with myself for not being able to do more to make it better.

As I sat and listened to the smart guy in the room, I felt even worse. I am his dad and I should be able to fix it, right? Almost within seconds of having the thought, the psychologist paused and asked, "Kris, do you have any questions?"

Panic overcame me momentarily. Had my thoughts really been my voice? Did I actually say what I had been thinking out loud? Focusing on his question and making sure my mouth wasn't moving, I thought, "I have more questions than you ever want to hear and I have more issues than you can even imagine." But instead I looked at him and said, "What can I do and how do I do it?"

I will never forget what he said to me, having total confidence in my ability.

"Kris, I need you to be you and help Will be Will."

That moment was defining for me. It was the birth of the thinking process I now call "Meeting Them Where They Are." I had no idea why the phrase came at that time. It was even years later before it became a way of life and focal point of our business. It simply means that each person has special and unique personality traits, habits and skills he develops over the course of his life. Most, if not all, make us who we are; they can determine our thoughts, behaviors, achievements or failures.

When attempting to help others in their time of need, it is

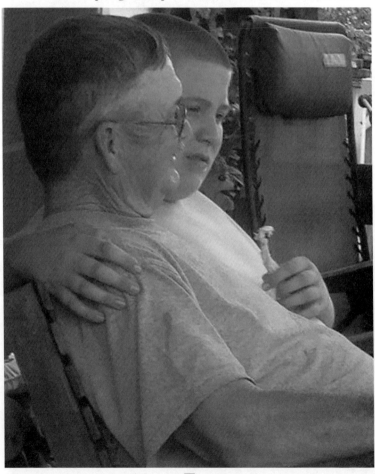

imperative for us to meet them where they are, not where we want or expect them to be. Although this lesson was learned in the context of Will, I have found it true in many aspects of life and with every person I have come in contact with.

If you have heard me speak, you have probably heard me say, "We do not put fourth graders in geometry for a reason, now do we?" The reasons are plenty; just to think we would sounds crazy. Yet, we make assumptions about others that can be just as foolish. We expect others to think, react or behave a certain way without considering, "Is this something the individual can really do? Are they capable? Do they have the skills, knowledge, experience and maturity to do so?"

It is illogical to even consider asking fourth graders to partake in geometry class unless they are academically well beyond the expected developmental age. But we find ourselves as parents asking our children to do or be things they are not yet capable of emotionally, behaviorally or academically. In classrooms our children are being held to expectations based on a scale, a chart created by a political committee's action without the consideration of the specific backgrounds, disabilities and life circumstances of the individuals those actions impact.

Even in our day-to-day life as adults, we often fail to consider where the person standing in front of us in the grocery line or sitting in the row behind us at church has been in life. We judge without thought. What if they have never been taught how to do what we expect? What if they do not understand the reason for an action, the "why not"?

My mind takes me back to April 2003, sitting in a small room on the campus of Arkansas Children's Hospital. That day will be forever etched in the memory bank of my mind. Not only was it a day that changed the course of life for my son forever, but it changed mine and all of our family, as well. That day was filled with much sadness and grief for our boy. Receiving Will's diagnosis was like a death sentence for the dreams we had for him since his birth. We felt like failures.

Knowing what I know now, I realize that we were not met where we were as his parents. No parent is ever prepared to hear the words "non-curable," "will never talk," and "be institutionalized" within a two minute span. These words were incomprehensible to us at that time.

Heck, before that day, I didn't even know what autism was except for what I had learned from the "Rain Man" movie. The expectation placed on us by doctors and therapists was nowhere near what we could handle.

We were allowed to walk away devastated for our child, feeling his life was over and ours sentenced to despair without hope. I beg of you, regardless of your professional position, your walk with Christ, your standing in the community, or your right to be human, never let anyone leave your presence without hope!

I look back on that day as a one of my worst hands down. It became a defining moment for me, one I never want to repeat. A defining moment because the word "quit" had never been in my vocabulary up to that point, but for a long season thereafter, it became a prominent and lingering word. I wanted to quit. I was overcome with the guilt of what I had done or not done to cause this ailment in my son. I was stricken over what would happen to him now.

Thankfully, there were those around me that "met me where I was." They refused to let me go down that road alone. Some days they joined me in sorrow and let me mope around in self-pity. Other days, they told me to pull myself up out of the black hole and fight—fight for my child's success and for my family because, disability or not, they were worth fighting for.

Everyone needs someone in his corner. We need people who will meet us where we are. My friends didn't just help me wrap my mind around the facts, they allowed me to feel the pain, the sorrow and death-like emotions of losing the dream I had of what my son would be like. Then they encouraged me to accept a new dream and realize that just because the plan had changed, the participant was still the same. My son was still my son, despite the autism, the label and the bleak future we had been led to believe confronted us.

And, boy, were those friends right! The guys that stood with me throughout that storm are still my friends today. They have continued to weather the storms with me and celebrate our successes. Why? Because they took the time to meet me where I needed to be met at a time I had no hope. They helped me get to where I needed to go in order to be the person I needed to be—for myself, my son and my family.

And look where we all are now! I will be forever thankful!

Families that consist of children with special needs have so much more going on than a traditional family could ever imagine. Their lives are entwined with myriad amounts of therapies, appointments, responsibilities and stress, more than one human should have to carry. Parents are often faced with financial struggles because only one parent works outside the home. They don't get enough sleep, and face medical and educational decisions no one should have to face. All that comes without an instruction manual, much like being a parent. It is a task you learn as you go and pray that you get right.

But when you are parenting a child with special needs the stakes are often higher, the playing field is uneven and the responsibilities endless. Although often self-imposed, many of these families have emotional issues to overcome such as guilt, denial, "super-parent syndrome," depression, anxiety, and fear—lots and lots of fear. Fear of the unknown, of others, of expectations. etc. Now include the other children of these families, the siblings of the disabled child. The dynamics within these families are so unequally balanced at times it is difficult to make sure the siblings receive the attention, care and guidance they need. Yet so often you will find they are more than willing to step aside for the sake of their brother or sister. Why? Because their family and others have learned to meet them where they are.

I could share story after story about our own life and others, how our paths turned out differently because someone was willing to "meet us where we were." Reflect on your life. Can you think of a time when someone came to your rescue? When someone met you where you were? When someone stepped in and did what you couldn't at the time? What about those times we look back on and wonder why no one extended a hand when we were at our lowest and just needed a friend?

My challenge to you is this: With every person you come into contact with—for the first time or on a daily basis—meet them where they are. See where they are. Have an open mind, an open heart and eyes of discernment. Are they hurting? Do they need someone in their corner? Do they need a smile, a sweet word of encouragement or someone to be their cheerleader for just a fleeting moment? Regardless of your walk in life, your profession, history, upbringing or family, life can be hard. God never promised us it was going to be easy. He only said he would be there. Often he uses others to be his hands and feet. Sometimes he uses us, when we listen and obey.

The humanity within our world has been misplaced due to the junk that has invaded it. We have lost the basic decency of being human, the art of bestowing kindness, love, patience, forgiveness and understanding to others. Instead we have begun to place unrealistic expectations on those who had no choice about where they landed in this world and, more often than not, those expectations have been placed on the kids in their lives.

For a moment reflect on your life. Do you see yourself and your life as easy or difficult? More blessed than cursed? Or is life a struggle you fight every day? Despite your answers, no one's life is perfect no matter what they may say. We still fight illnesses. We have bills to pay, dogs who bark and babies who cry, and those extra pounds or wrinkles we wish we didn't have.

Many of us would say we are definitely blessed more than we deserve, while others may feel we got slighted in this thing called life. Regardless of our current state, the world owes us nothing, but as human beings we owe it to ourselves, to one another and especially to our children, to extend a helping hand along the road of life. Meet each person where they are, even if it is not where they should be, or want to stay.

Be human.

Be kind.

Love people.

See the good in everyone.

Extend a hand to those in need, despite if you think they deserve it or not. It takes very little effort to point out someone's faults, but great skill to point out their success.

What are you doing? Are you building others up by meeting them where they are? Or are you standing above them while tearing them further down? The amazing thing is, you get to decide. You get to decide the impact you will make on others, your co-workers, your spouse, your family. You decide how you will take on the day. You have the choice of providing hope in someone's journey. You.

8
SECOND CHANCE KIDS

Most of us go through our lives having been given chance after chance after chance. We probably have been given chances we will never deserve. I know I've been given second chances—more than I deserve. I'm very grateful for a second chance, especially when a police officer turns on his lights and comes up talk to me about my speed. I'm very thankful for those times I have been given a chance to slow down and not received a ticket to the police ball or the county fair.

In this chapter, I want to share the amazing stories of just a few kiddos and adults I have had the priviledge of encountering. Some have received multiple chances to get things right, and oh, how it affected them and their parents. Due to the delicate nature of their stories, names have been changed.

The first individual is Sara Beth. Sara Beth is a preteen, and that brings an array of issues to everyone's existence. It is a rough time for anybody of that age, but especially for one in the spectrum of autism. She has a wonderful family—a great mom and dad and little sister— who will do everything they can to try make life work. Sara Beth has great people at school, therapists, teachers and paraprofessionals. Although the village can be amazing, issues and problems still arise.

I got the privilege of being called in to try to help and make things better for Sarah Beth. All of her caregivers and staff wanted help so I gave them some tips and some things that they can do. In the fall, we saw some tremendous progress with her moving buildings and we were able to get more communication out of her. She had some great help with some good people who were willing to do whatever needed to be done.

Everyone was at the end of their rope when I arrived. There were many discussions about what to do, and I get that, but I knew that I knew that I knew we just had to help her get through puberty, and it's hard to make it! It is hard for any teenager, but when it is someone who is on the spectrum, it is even tougher. In a case like Sara Beth, we had to stick it out and figure it out. We got some communication from Sara Beth, but not much other than her being able to move. Sometimes we just

have to wait the storm out. Everybody's got to hang tight and be on the same page.

Just to let you know, Sarah Beth is doing pretty good now! The family is getting better and better and I think mom and dad are doing better! We are just getting there and it takes a village to do it. I am just so thankful that I get to be a part of her life and family! Sara Beth, I love you and always will! One day you will read this and say, "That's me! I am doing so well!"

The next example is John. He has big-time issues. I guess I was concerned about his grandparents having a tough time. They did not really trust anybody and did not really want to do anything for anybody. This was one of the hardest cases I have ever worked on, but that little fella needed a lot of loving. I needed to take a deep breath and he needed an opportunity. I wanted to give him that opportunity. It was a very cool thing with him because I needed to give him that chance and he needed to give me the opportunity to work it out with him.

Today I see that kid in the hall and sometimes give him a high-five as he is walking to class. He's doing amazing! What is so cool is that somebody took the time to get on his level, where he lived, and worked to get him to where we want him to go! It is an amazing journey. The kid that may not have changed now has a chance because a person did something to help. I am just so glad to have been part of the solution!

Another individual I want to introduce you to is JJ. He was a very young little guy that I got to work with in his classroom. He had several difficulties that were determined to hinder his ability to control a lot of stuff. I got called in to see if I could help figure out how to attack these difficulties. JJ was a very smart and loving little boy and he took to me pretty well. After several weeks of figuring out meds, sleep patterns, environment and other structure things, I had a revelation I wanted to explore.

The issues we were trying to work on all happened in the afternoon of his day. I asked his teacher if he was eating lunch during the day because we had tried adjusting some of the medication times, but changing the times alone made no significant difference. The teacher said she was not sure if JJ was eating lunch because she did not go to lunch with her class. I spoke with the nurse about medications JJ was taking because food or lack of food intake can make a big difference in how these react inside the body. Then I learned JJ was not eating lunch—and food in the stomach was important for the meds JJ was taking and for his overall health.

With this information, the only thing I asked them to change was to make sure he ate lunch before taking his meds and that he ate enough for his size and weight. Within three days, we saw a significant behavior shift. JJ was much happier and most of the issues subsided. It was a very simple fix, yet it took us a while to figure it out. All things are possible and there is a solution if we look long enough and we keep trying things together!

The next individual we will call Lucas. Lucas has many issues in his life, from home to environment to social issues. He is probably the most challenging individual I have ever had the pleasure of working with in my career. Lucas is a virtual Houdini. If the power grid ever goes down, I am going to find him and have him live with me forever because he is amazing. Probably too smart for his own good at the time, but the sky is the limit for him. He has so many skills, yet lacks the social aspect of things because of the challenges he has had to face. Yet, you have to look beyond those things into what can or could be. I am so glad someone in my life looked beyond what was and
what saw what could be, and kept encouraging and loving me. The obstacles are many and the answers are few, yet we still try to do all we can together to make this precious soul have a chance to make it better than he found it years ago. Time will tell and we will not quit until it is finished.

Then there is Ann. When I was first introduced to Ann, she was a very young child with a multitude of issues. She seemed to have real difficulty working within the confines of even the smallest classrooms. Although difficult to help, she seemed to really take a liking to me and would do a lot of what I requested from her. As most of the kids I get to work with do, they seem to do really well with me. Perhaps it is because I am a dad and these kids need a positive male influence in their lives. Ann made a lot of strides over the several years I had the privilege to work with her, even though later she was transferred to a different provider, one could meet her every day needs and better prepare her for the future. It was a difficult thing to see and do, but in the end, it is all about helping kids be the best they can be.

Last but not least is Taylor. Taylor is his real name, by the way. Taylor started helping us with Will right after Taylor had graduated from high school. Taylor had just turned eighteen and was helping us during the summer before his freshman year of college. His major was Kinesiology and I think he wanted to be a coach. He was a pretty good football player in high school. He and Will hit it off, but they had their ups and downs, too, just like brothers!

After working with Will for a year, Taylor decided to change his major to special education. Now, remember Will is non-verbal and does not say a lot, but if he talks we all listen. Taylor was no exception with Will and they became best buddies. Taylor helped us and Will through many of the trials of becoming a teenager and beyond. He did things with and for Will that we appreciate to this day. He graduated after five years of college and went on to become a self-contained teacher in northwest Arkansas.

I asked Taylor after his first or second semester of teaching this question: "If you had to say which one taught you more about how to teach and manage your classroom would it be working with Will or your degree?"

He replied, "Will taught me more than I ever learned in a classroom to be able to help kids!"

—

This about the kid they told me would never speak and would be in an institution by age twelve. Taylor still comes to visit when he is in town and Will still loves him to death. My girls love it when he comes, too, because he became our family. Taylor comes from a long line of families helping families and individuals with special needs. He has no real idea the impact he made on Will or the rest of us, and we have yet to see to the fullest what kind of impact was made on Taylor. Taylor loves big and has a huge heart. You cannot teach that, but you can sure work with it. He will be forever etched with a spot in our family and in Will's life.

These are just a couple examples of the impact that a non-verbal individual has had on lives that he may never even meet. Because of the multiple chances I have been given and have taken, others have benefitted and had a chance to succeed. There are many who have walked, are walking and will walk with me along the way. I get lots of accolades, but it is truly the ones in the trenches every day who deserve the praise. They do what most won't for those who need it the most.

We all need multiple chances every day. What are you doing to make that happen? What am I doing? We all can do more and better so we should.

9
LIGHT FROM
A DIFFERENT
PERSPECTIVE

If you have been around the block a few times (as the old saying goes), you realize that in any situation there are as many opinions as there are people. As we age, we tend to see viewpoints from the younger generation's as less important or lacking validity and value. It is often foolish of us to be this way; some of the greatest insights come from those with less experience and fewer jaded views. If you have been around me, you know one of my favorite quotes is, "You have to get under the desk," meaning, in the school realm, if a kiddo gets under the desk, you get under the desk with him. In everyday life it is the equivalent of meeting others where they are, not judging or criticizing where they are or how they got there.

Have you ever been under the desk? Looking back can you see a time in your life when you desperately needed someone to come to you, crawl under that desk with you and tell you it will be okay? Or perhaps you can visualize a time when you should have been the one to reach out to someone else. How can we, as followers of Christ and even kind humans, understand the dynamics of empathy or have an understanding

—

of other's trials unless we have been there?

In this chapter I want to share with you insights from siblings of children on the spectrum. I feel this will give you an unabridged view of life as a sibling to a child on the spectrum. Some of these responses will cause your heart to break and then soar within a matter of words. Open your heart, listen and learn, remember these are children, just like yours who are traveling a path they were placed on by no decision of their own. There are some pretty powerful messages at work here, messages of hope, undeniable love and devotion, and often unfathomable acceptance from siblings who without a doubt have every reason to be jealous, resentful or bitter about their situation. And yet here they are, baring their heart and soul to help others understand. My hope is that you listen.

Question 1: What is the one thing that you love about having a sibling with autism?

Kate, 15 years old, older brother:

"It has taught me to look at life in a new perspective. You can't judge something you see or that is happening by just looking at it and assuming. You have to know and understand the circumstances of the situation."

Kylen, 10 years old, older brother:

"It has made me tough, more patient and understanding."

Emma, 18 years old, younger brother:

"I think the thing I love the most about having a sibling with autism is that I have a unique perspective on the world and the people in it. There is this community, almost like a hidden treasure, that is filled with these miracle children with special needs. They do not look like regular kids and certainly do not act like regular kids. That being said, they are so special and loving. Some of them are smarter than the people we consider 'geniuses.' These special needs children are creative and perfect in their own special way. Their families have learned to push through adversities and struggles along with their children, and have overcome some big hurdles. You will just never meet a community that is more driven and open to seeing the beauty in the little things than this group of families. If I did not have a sibling with a special need, I would have probably never met the families I have met or learned the kind of acceptance that I have. And I love that. The fact is this one disorder has affected my life that much."

Karleigh, 10 years old, older sister:

"One thing I love about having a sibling with autism is you can't fight with them (because she can't talk to me)."

Dawson, 17 years old, older brother:

—
85

"He is the most loving little thing in the world."

Daxton, 8 year old, younger brother:
  "I love that he is sweet and honorable in his own way."

Anna Claire, 5 years old, twin older brothers:
  "They are sweet."

Question 2: **What is the worst thing about having a sibling with autism?**
  "Probably everyone always looking at you with a look of disgust. Also, when you tell someone that your sibling has autism, they look at you in a whole new way like something about you has changed." (Kate)

  "Have you ever made a new friend and you had to explain your whole life story so that the one small thing that you did that seemed a little odd made sense and didn't seem so strange? That is what having a sibling with autism is like on a daily basis. I would say that the "worst" thing about having a sibling with autism is having to try to acclimate everyone you come in contact with to the fact that your brother is not like a normal kid. Although it is getting better, we do not live in a world where it is socially acceptable to have a mental or social disorder that causes you to not behave like everyone else. So, in addition to conditioning your sibling to other people, you have to prepare and explain to people the whole situation and pray that maybe they will keep the looks of disgust and pointing fingers and snickers and stares away and just give you a little bit of a break.
  We are really all trying our best to make this as enjoyable and pleasant for everyone as possible. People do not know this, but they make our families, at least in my opinion, feel like an inconvenience. I am sorry that my brother made a loud screeching noise. I am sorry that we have paper all around our

table. I am sorry that if the pizza is not cut a certain way and we will not take it. We did not ask for a brother/son with autism. But God gave us this road to walk and so we tightened our laces and got to walking. So I guess the worst part is honestly just feeling as though you are inconveniencing others around you." (*Emma*)

"I can't go outside and play with her like other siblings can." (*Karleigh*)

"Worst thing would probably be when he is insanely wild." (*Dawson*)

"All he does is play on his game all the time, and does not seem interested in doing my things very often." (*Daxton*)

"It is embarrassing when he gets upset and everyone stares." (*Kylen*)

"My brother hits me sometimes." (*Anna Claire*)

Question 3: How do you think your life would be different without a sibling with autism?
"I can't answer. I never think about not have a sibling with autism and could never think about it. Being a sibling to someone who has autism will always be a part of me and I would never change it." (*Kate*)

"I was around four years old when my brother was diagnosed, so I have very few memories of him before, meaning that, for the majority of my life, I have not known anything different. I love my brother, even with his diagnosis, and I would not trade our troubles for the world because I know that it has made me who I am today. But to say that I have not thought about how my life would be different would be a lie. Of course I have thought about it. In my head, I would have grown up with a brother who played with trucks and mud and annoyed me and who would grow up to play sports and protect me from guys that were rude, and would be a total ladies' man. My life would have probably been easier growing up. With all that being said, as 'perfect' as that may sound, I would not trade my life or the experiences I have been through with my "little" brother for any kind of fairytale story you could have come up with." (*Emma*)

"There would not be as much love in our family." (*Karleigh*)

"I would not be able to understand people with autism and how it is like to live with someone with that condition." (*Dawson*)

"My life would be boring, because I like how he is." (*Daxton*)

Question 4: What is one thing you would want those who don't have a sibling with autism to know?
"Looking, pointing, and making fun of someone who has autism is just cruel. They can't help that they were born with autism. Instead of making fun of them for their disability, help them work through it. I mean how would you feel if you walked around and people looked, pointed, and made fun of you? Not so good, would it? Also, to the siblings, it absolutely infuriates them to death. I can't stand it when people do that." (*Kate*)

"I want to take a moment to address the people reading this book who have no relation to a person with autism. You were not raised like I was and I want you all to know that I can understand how this may all seem kind of crazy and foreign. But here is a tip that I have for you that will help you guys understand us a little bit more: You really do not know what it is like unless you experience it firsthand. Our life is crazy and chaotic and not simple. So many variables play in to our daily life." (*Emma*)

"That you do not say, 'the autistic girl.' You say, 'the girl with autism.' Or even call them by their name." (*Karleigh*)

"People should know not to take their siblings for granted.

While he is not severe it is still difficult to do things that normal brothers would do." (*Dawson*)

"They should know that you should treat people who are different than you nice, and be polite because we need to show we care even though they are different." (Daxton)

"My brother is funny; he says random things that makes us laugh all the time, like singing commercials." (*Kylen*)

"They like to play with me." (*Anna Claire*)

Question 5: What is something that your sibling has taught you over your life?
"That no matter what, nothing can stop you from reaching the stars. My brother is a great and amazing kid that hasn't let autism stop him." (*Kate*)

"Having a brother with autism has taught me some of the biggest life lessons. I think the biggest thing I have learned is how to find joy and triumph in the little things. Not many people get excited by your sibling saying your name for the first time, or him being able to sit through one of your games, or even when your sibling just puts his seatbelt on and leaves it on for the entire car ride. In my opinion, those are things to find excitement in! Like, hey, today we progressed. Today we did a little better than yesterday. Without him even knowing it, he has taught me how to enjoy my life no matter what is thrown my way; how to overcome adversity, and how to always persevere." (*Emma*)

"She has taught me not to sweat the small stuff in life." (*Karleigh*)

"He has probably taught me to take a different perspective

of people because you never know what it is like in their world." (*Dawson*)

"He has taught me that autistic kids are loving, sweet and gentle. We should accept people who are different, and treat them the way we treat non-autistic people." (*Daxton*)

"To be loud." (*Anna Claire*)

"To be more patient and understanding." (*Kylen*)

Question 6: What is one thing that you have learned that has helped you help others who might not understand?

"One thing is that I ask them to look at it like they were in the kid with autism's shoes. It makes them realize that it is not nice to do things to others that you would not want done to you and also that they would want someone to stick up for them." (*Kate*)

"Having a brother with autism has helped me learn tolerance and understanding. It has not always been easy and I have learned how to take a step back and take it one step at a time. This knowledge and life skill helps me with those people who do not know what it is like. I am able to take my tolerance and apply it to the other side of the equation. When people ask questions that to me may seem obvious or insulting, I take a step back and remind myself that they haven't seen or dealt with what my family has and they just do not know. I try to use the life lessons Will has taught me to help educate those who ask me about him and autism." (*Emma*)

"I have helped others to not be afraid." (*Karleigh*)

"I have learned to take it easy and choose my battles because some of them won't end well." (*Dawson*)

—

"Even though people are different, you should still treat them the way you want others to treat you. All of us really have something 'different' about us." (*Daxton*)

"Just because someone is different doesn't mean they are weird." (*Kylen*)

Question 7: What role has autism played in your relationship with your sibling?

"A sibling with autism changes the way we are around each other because we don't have the same bond as I have with my other siblings. We have different ways of connecting with each other, like cooking his favorite meals and stuff." (*Kate*)

"Having a younger brother with autism has changed how we are around each other because, like previously stated, it is not the normal kind of sister/brother stuff. I have had to teach him things that are different from what most older sisters have to, plus I look out for him in a different capacity as well." (*Emma*)

"It is like a barrier that is hard to break through. But I am willing to break through that barrier." (*Karleigh*)

"Autism has helped grow a more loving relationship. Bad things might happen but he always loves me no matter what." (*Dawson*)

"Autism has reversed our relationship in the knowledge that although I am the younger brother, I know that I will always take care of my older brother." (*Daxton*)

"It is sometimes embarrassing. He gets upset and others don't understand and so they think he is weird and that I am weird." (*Kylen*)

"It makes me sad. One of my brothers hits me, but my other brother is my best friend." (*Anna Claire*)

Question 8: Are there times when you have felt slighted, overlooked, jealous or resentful of your sibling? If so, what situations caused that and how did you handle it?
"No, I never really have before. I have always understood there are different circumstances when it comes to taking care of my brother. My parents have always done the best to treat us all the same." (*Kate*)

"This is a hard question for me to answer truthfully because the answer is yes. I do not want any of my parents to feel like they have done the wrong thing by how they have taken care of him, but, yeah, there are times that I have felt overlooked. Resentful is not the right word, but overlooked. It is just that there have been times when what my brother wants has been the priority or making sure he is taken care of is more important than me, which sounds selfish and, honestly, kind of is. That is what has 'reeled' me back in, the fact that I am actually capable of taking care of myself and that I was just being selfish." (*Emma*)

"Yes! When I have felt like my parents are spending more time with my sister. But I told my parents and they explained we both get time with our parents. It's just in different ways (like I get to do activities that my sister can't, like dance class, piano, shopping trips, etc.)." (*Karleigh*)

"I have sometimes felt jealous of him because it seems that he just has an easier life, but growing older it seems like it is more of a struggle than I thought." (*Dawson*)

"Sometimes he seems to get his way more than me, and I feel like they care more about him." (*Daxton*)

—
93

"I often get jealous. My brother gets stuff all the time because no one wants him upset. I get angry sometimes because we have to go to therapy all the time for him." (*Kylen*)

"They get a lot of attention all the time." (*Anna Claire*)

Question 9: How has your sibling's disability affected your family, positively and negatively?
"My brother was diagnosed when I was very young. I have never known any different than the way my family is." (Kate)

"The weird part about answering this question is that I assume it has impacted and changed my family, but I really wouldn't know the difference because for my entire life, at least as much of it as I can remember, has been with a brother with autism. I could list how positively we have bonded and became a stronger unit, and how negatively we have had to deal with different obstacles, and our family is definitely not the traditional one. But in all honesty, I do not know anything different." (*Emma*)

"It brought us closer together, and negatively, lots of crying when she hurts someone." (*Karleigh*)

"I think it has positively affected the family. He gives a sense of compassion that helps bring a family together. He does not stop loving and I think that is something that will always be positive to a family." (*Dawson*)

"Having a person with autism makes our family different, and different is always good." (*Daxton*)

"My brother hurts my mom, dad and me all the time." (*Kylen*)

"We stay busy all the time because of we are always having to go places for them, and my mom has to clean all the time." (*Anna Claire*)

Question 10: Do you think having a sibling with a disability has made you a better person? Why?
"Obviously! Without my brother, I would not love as much, care as much, be as patient, as kind, have as big of heart, and be the person I am today." (*Kate*)

"Oh, for sure, without a doubt. I am who I am today because of this disability and how it has affected me and my family. I am who I am because of all the things we have had to deal with and all the lessons he has taught me." (*Emma*)

"Yes! It has made me nicer and more patient." (*Karleigh*)

"I think it has made me a better person. I can better understand that people have it way differently than I do, and it gives me an insight that life can be difficul,t but what you make out of it that can be wonderful." (*Dawson*)

"Having a sibling with autism helps me to understand that it is important to treat all people nice, no matter their disability." (*Daxton*)

"I am a much more understanding person and I am very nice." (*Kylen*)

"I love them a lot." (*Anna Claire*)

Wow! These kids told it like it is. If you want to leave things better than you found it, just pay attention to what these siblings have said. I personally feel this was very insightful and makes me appreciate our journey more than ever, seeing that we are making a difference. Knowing that not only do we as parents feel like our child with autism has made us better, it has made their siblings better too. Sometimes we get so caught up in focusing on our destination, we overlook our journey.

How are you viewing your journey? Is it being overlooked because you are too focused on the prize per say? It is up to us to shine the light, to make our circumstances better and those around us better. We should always leave things better than we found them. As adults, as parents, educators or humans, we have the ability to make a difference in those around us. Will we use what we have been blessed with, or will we say, "Not me"?

The choice is ours to make. Choose wisely!

10
MANY FACES
AND PLACES

W ith the addition of the twins to our family of five, there were many things we did not foresee happening or could have ever adequately prepared for. Looking back, it is amazing to see how the hand of God orchestrated even the smallest details of our lives and allowed us to be a part of it—both unexplainable miracles and trials which brought forth fruit after the hard work.

The twins were preemies and, although not in imminent danger at birth, their early and abrupt entrance to the world did cause some issues. Who better to tackle some of these special issues than people who deal with special needs on a daily basis at home and on the job? I often wonder if God has more faith in my ability than I do.

Rather still, I press on with the task that he has placed before me with humbleness and boldness. We could foresee many challenges, but amazingly, there were some Will and others helped us with.

Within weeks of the twins joining our home, Chance became very ill during the middle of the night. Brandi rushed him to Arkansas Children's Hospital while I remained home with our other children. Her trip there was filled with prayer as we pleaded with God to touch the child we had so quickly grown to love. Upon arrival, he was rushed to a room with a team of doctors yelling out orders. They plugged him up to all sorts of equipment. Overwhelmed by the sudden turn of events, Brandi stood strong as she watched and waited for what we would later find out was the fight of his life.

After things settled we learned Chance had RSV, which is a danger to all children of young age, but with Chance's premature lungs it was almost fatal. The virus had attacked his body and had decreased his oxygen production to the point of being blue when Brandi arrived at the emergency room with him that night. One ER doctor told us that if Chance had arrived five minutes later, he might not have made it.

Once stable enough to be moved, he was placed in PICU where he remained for almost two weeks. Heavily sedated, hooked up to more wires than you can imagine, we were faced with the overwhelming emotions of almost losing a child we felt God had sent our way.

Throughout the night and early morning, Brandi had been alone. As she was able to make phone call, our village begin to appear. We had those who helped with our kids at home, visited us in the hospital, and many who stayed shifts so Brandi could see the other kids at home, shower and change. I stayed as much in one place or the other while continuing to work every day. This little hiccup in our lives lasted for three weeks. After his two weeks in PICU, Chance was moved to a regular room before being dismissed. We spent our first Easter with the twins in the hospital.

Although privy to some information regarding his birth and post-delivery, we were not aware how seriously under-developed his lungs were. It wasn't until after his hospital stay that we were made aware of just how close our little fellow had actually come to not surviving. Hearing the news of our child's recent brush with death moved us to a place of gratitude we

had never experienced before. We will forever be indebted to
ACH for their care of Chance during such a traumatic time. They
made us feel like we were at home, assisting us with all of our
needs, even ones we didn't even know we had.

We are blessed to have this hospital so close and available
whenever our kids needed care. Fortunately we were
surrounded by friends, family and hospital staff who stepped

in to help us make the best decisions possible regarding all of our children. We could not have done any of this without them. They kept Myracle and Will, stayed at the hospital with Chance when we needed them, and made sure we ate and got the rest we needed, too. Having a child with special needs like Will and having two newly placed infant twins, it is very difficult to coordinate things at times. We were beyond grateful and humbled to have a vast number of people in our corner who helped us.

This was only one of the numerous obstacles Chance would encounter during the first year of his life. After his knockout round with the RSV, he continued to face an uphill battle. He was failing to meet his normal developmental milestones, and we were becoming more concerned with his lack of interaction. Taking our concerns to heart, we begin exploring different avenues as to what could be causing the lack of growth developmentally, physically and educationally. Through therapy evaluations and many doctor appointments, we discovered he had hearing and vision issues. The poor kid couldn't see or hear, bless his heart. It is difficult to have interaction when you can't see or hear. But oh was the little guy cute in his glasses! From the moment we put them on his face, his eyes lit up! It was obvious he was seeing things for the first time. It was one of those moments you live for as a parent, but at the time you want to beat yourself up for not realizing there was a problem or getting help sooner.

Despite the frustration and guilt, we once again had to rely on our faith and our village to work out all the kinks. They provided support to not only our other children, but to Brandi and me.

After seeing improvements with his vision, we continued our search for answers regarding his hearing. After several failed hearing exams, his Ear Nose and Throat doctor at Children's Hospital decided to be proactive. He scheduled him for surgery to put tubes in his ears despite the lack of recurrent ear infections. We felt so blessed to have a doctor who listened to our concerns even when there was no diagnosis to back up our claims. As parents, sometimes you just know when something isn't right, and luckily God had placed the doctor Chance needed.

Since birth, Chance had issues with what was thought to have been acid reflux. We had been treating it since before his bout with RSV, which had been contributed to his aspiration. During this procedure, the ENT was also going to check his sinus cavity, throat, and lungs to see if other problems existed .

With all this on our plate, prayer was often our only refuge. I was up the night before praying for the procedure the next day looking for comfort and answers. As I prayed, I begin to feel an overwhelming presence that it was going to be okay. That it was all going to be okay. Feeling this assurance, I awoke Brandi and told her I was convinced Chance would no longer need his glasses after the next day's surgery. Yes, you read that right. *His glasses.*

Yes, I know, his surgery was on his ears and throat, but

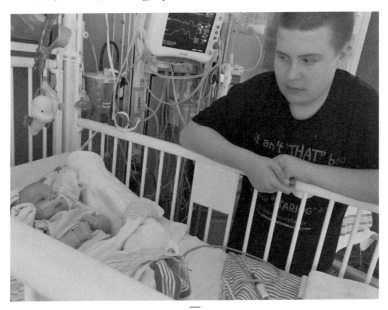

I felt a peace about it all, just like what we often pray for, a "peace that passes all understanding." I have experienced God's ultimate comfort several times in my life and this was definitely a time I needed His assurance. As always, he came through.

Chance's surgery went great. Tubes were placed, excess skin causing his floppy airway was removed, and we were confident his hearing would be restored completely.

And his vision? Yep, sure enough, after a couple of weeks Chance begin removing his glasses constantly, throwing them off, refusing to let us put them on (as much as an infant could). Because he had not displayed resistance to his glasses before, we began to question if they were hurting him, or perhaps had his vision changed? We made a return visit to his pediatric ophthalmologists to have him examined. The doctor conducted a thorough exam due to our concerns. Upon completion, she stated her findings. The glasses were no longer needed.

Brandi in typical form, began her mama bear-style questioning: "How could this happen? Was he misdiagnosed in the beginning? Did his glasses fix it?"

The doctor responded, "I have no idea what has happened, but I would say it was a miracle."

Chills ran all over me as I heard her say, "I have no idea," meaning that, medically, there was no explanation. I looked at Brandi and said, "I knew it!" God had heard our pleas and had answered our prayers to take care of our little one.

I think at times, we all feel the move of God in our life. Sometimes it is the still small voice, other times it may just be a feeling or impression. It can often leave you wondering, "Is this real? Am I dreaming or perhaps just hearing things?" But this was no dream! Our little guy's eyesight had been restored, as well as his hearing. I always say you can believe what you will, but I know what I know. This time there was no denying what had happened and it was a true miracle!

Throughout many of these life stories shared, we have mentioned a couple that have played a vital part in our life and

the life of our children, especially the twins. Let me introduce you to them. Scott and I had become friends in college. In recent years we found ourselves living in the same town. Brandi had gotten to know his wife, Shannon, when they worked together in a small district outside of our town. They have four boys which includes a set of twins. Scott and I reconnected these years later, and Shannon and Brandi had worked together for a brief time; that was really as far as our relationship had gone.

All of their children were teenagers at the time, and although we had teens as well our paths just didn't really cross— until Tuesday, the day after we got the twins. Our school district was having a millage vote to build a new elementary school. Wanting to support children and the school district, Brandi made this her first official outing with two infants. Wanting to make sure her vote was counted, she set off to the local sports complex to vote. Since the twins had been with us less than twenty-four hours, no one outside of family knew what had transpired. In true Brandi fashion, she garnered attention as she walked in with not just one car seat and infant, but two car seats with two infants, and boy/girl twins nonetheless.

Obviously this got attention. Having twins, period, seems to grab attention, but having twins appear out of thin air gets you a lot of attention! Scott was there and asked the questions others were notably thinking, yet not saying out loud.

"Where did these come from?"

As Brandi explained, he requested he watch them for a minute to allow her to go vote emptyhanded. The rest is history. They are now known as Uncle Scott and Aunt Shannon, or as the twins say, "Nannon." Their family has embraced ours as we have them, and their boys are like extra siblings to mine now. It's amazing and often confusing to others how our two families have joined but yet aren't related.

God's plan is always perfect. What could have been a bad situation for twins, God turned into something amazing, touching countless lives in the process.

I would be amiss if I didn't mention this story to you as well when sharing with you the most notable things that have impacted our lives since the last book. Will is an amazing young man and has made many accomplishments over the years, despite his autism, but none of them have been possible without the help of our village. Sometimes our village is brought in by our invitation; others have become a part of our village by request or urgency.

One of those was the band director while Will was in junior high. She was Will's bus driver and, although he was the first one off the route, she had gotten to know him pretty well. One day we received a call from her with an unusual request. She wanted to know if we had ever considered giving Will a shot at band. I think Brandi and I both were in shock. No, we had never considered it and were humbled that anyone else had, much less the director.

She explained her ideas and asked if we would be willing to give it a go. She assured us she would contact us if any issues arose, but she really wanted to give it a try. We excitedly, yet cautiously, agreed.

Not only was Will able to participate in the junior high band period as her assistant, he showed such an interest in playing that he was given the option of choosing an instrument. And of all things for a child with autism to play (who are known for often having issues with loud noises), he chose drums. Yes, you read that correctly. He wanted to play the drums. Go big or go home, huh, Will? I think that is his motto in many things. He immediately joined the beginner percussion class to learn how to play the snare drum.

Although we never had the opportunity to witness Will playing due to the obvious embarrassment of parents showing up where they don't belong, she kept us abreast of his progress. It was startling when people saw Will, who stood heads taller than his classmates. However, the young people worked with

—

him and included him in everything they were doing.

The director told how, in the beginning when he first joined the class, Will started out in the back of the room, just watching. But as time went on and at the encouragement of those in the class, he had progressed towards the middle of the class, surrounded by his classmates as they worked with him right along with the staff.

This process was such an eye opening experience for not only Brandi and me, but for so many others. It spoke volumes to us of the caliber of teachers we have within our school district. It let us know the administration was on board with this special lady's request. It was nice as parents to have others want him included without having to beg or demand it, and rewarding to know that he was meeting the expectations that were set before him.

Just think. Without the insistence of his band director, we may have not agreed to this great journey.

I could share so many stories and shout outs to people who have proven a vital part of our village. Although we are unable to list or share them all, you know who you are. We have been in so many places with Will and the twins and have seen so many faces of hope and encouragement that we could never begin to show enough gratitude.

Always remember, no matter how big or how small of a part you have played in our lives and the lives of our children, what you have done will never be forgotten. We think about our blessings every day and pray that we or our kiddos have touched your lives as you have touched ours.

11
PIECES OF
THE PUZZLE

Almost a year to the day before Brandi called me with news of the twins, she had undergone a total hysterectomy. It wasn't something she wanted, but was imperative for her health and sanity (and more so for ours). The hysterectomy devastated her, to put it mildly. She had believed since her teen years that God was going to give her a baby despite years of female issues, and she had never wavered in her belief. Since being married, we had taken steps to increase our chances of having our own little one, though it never worked out like we had hoped and prayed.

Although yearning for a baby, Brandi had mothered my children as her own since we met. Now young adults, Emma, Will and Kate could not be loved more by her, yet she still struggled with not having a child that was "ours," as she puts it.

Throughout our journey together we have learned many things, but God has shown us his promises are true, his timing is perfect and all he asks us to do is believe, wait and listen. Our very own "Myracle" and second "Chance" entered our home in March 2015, and what we thought would be a short term stay of fifteen to thirty days became sixty, ninety, then 120 days.

—

Brandi's sister, the biological mother of Myracle and Chance, found herself in trouble with legal issues. She desperately wanted to turn her life around, but knew that doing so would take time. She placed her twins with us, believing we would give them the protection and love she could not provide at that time. The guardianship became a more permanent solution than we had ever imagined. The story of God's grace in her life and ours could be the subject of another whole book!

Throughout this journey, our main concern was how the babies (often referred to as the "twins") would affect Will, our son with autism. If you know anything about Autism Spectrum Disorders, you know that routine, schedules and consistency are a main staple in the lives of those on the spectrum. There is nothing about babies, much less two babies, that is routine, scheduled or consistent. Each baby had its own schedule and was not in sync with the other one—or anyone else's schedule, for that matter. Research and autism professionals will tell you this is a horrifying combination, one that likely would not work to the betterment of Will or his progress.

But oh how they are wrong!

Within weeks, Will began to blossom into a young man we didn't even know existed. He took ownership of the twins and made it his duty to protect them. He alerted us when one would cry, and give us "what for" when he thought we were doing something wrong. His behavior at school improved, his communication increased and his awareness heightened. He had not only accepted his new role of big brother, but was embracing and thriving in it.

The more I analyzed our situation, the more alarmed I became. What if the twins got sick? Both had some health issues due to their premature and traumatic birth and would need medical assistance for some time.

What if someone showed up trying to claim them? We would have no way to get the help they needed because we had no legal right to them at all. The more I thought about this, the

—

more I realized these were no longer "the good ole days." These were the days of HIPPA, privacy acts and legal guardianship. It became evident that in order to care for the twins as we had been entrusted, we needed to take steps to legally solidify our responsibility.

We obtained an attorney and started the process to gain guardianship. We petitioned the courts, and with the support of their biological mom, our petition went through without a hitch. With that hurdle under our belt, we found ourselves beginning to plan more for them and their future than we had ever thought we would (especially me). God's hand is often so evident that we sometimes wonder how we could ever doubt the God we serve and his sovereignty. Within weeks we knew we had done the right thing. Chance had been admitted to Arkansas Children's Hospital in Little Rock with RSV where he stayed almost three weeks. We marveled at God's divine wisdom prompting us to have the forethought of obtaining guardianship before we were in desperate need.

At some point during this beautiful chaos, we began to see how these children were being woven into our lives permanently. I could go on for days about how God lines everything up perfectly—from the easy transfer of doctors, openings for two infants at the local daycare, to running into Scott and Shannon the day after their arrival. Every detail just seemed to fall into place, which we know isn't just coincidence. Thanking God every step of the way and knowing he is working on our behalf is a very humbling experience. Seeing the entire picture years later, I can only praise him for being the big God he is. I stand in awe of how he worked everything out, even to the minutest of details.

After several months, we began to realize that what we thought was going to be a short little stay, might turn into forever. We were all okay with it. Taking a very deep breath or two, we finally started talking about adopting them and making it truly a family of seven. (Yes, you can smile or laugh right here,

—
113

but if you know me you can see me doing the deep breaths!)

God was steadily working unbeknownst to us, lining up everything perfectly to make a lengthy process into a very simple and short course. Feeling like the entire situation was a "God directed thing," we made the decision to adopt after getting input from our three older children, close friends and family.

Having a lawyer in the family is always helpful when approaching the legal system. My cousin, LeAnne, represented us, and although it seemed to take forever, we finally had our court date in April 2016. As in all the times before, God had gone before us and prepared the way.

In all honesty, I am not very patient and the judge does not work on my time frame, I can assure you. As we sat and waited anxiously, we were informed that the judge assigned to our case was not coming in that day, but another one would take cases as he could. We were aggravated to say the least.

At first LeAnne told me that this could mean a continuance. We sat and waited and waited. We waited with two fifteen-month-old babies who were crawling and trying to walk everywhere. We waited with a teen with severe autism. We waited with two very bored teen girls. We waited for what seemed like forever.

Then our names were called.

We had a crowd of supporters with us in the courtroom. Due of the long wait, both twins were asleep and everyone else was a little disheveled. After swearing us in, our lawyer made the judge aware of our situation (Will and his noises). Then the judge began to ask questions, which we answered without hesitation.

Within a few minutes, the judge granted our petition for adoption that would be final in six months. It was one of the best days of my life! Our children and extended family were with us to welcome the final two pieces to the puzzle of our family.

—

During the adoption process, we had many ask if we were going to change their names. At first the names Myracle and Chance did seem a little different. When people asked us their names, they would always give you the "hmm" or the "oh, that is different" (you knew what they were really thinking), or they would assume we named them that because we were old. So it surprised them to learn that their biological mom named them. And though I wasn't crazy about their names at first, I came to believe she knew they were going to be "our Myracle and Second Chance."

At two years of age, we cannot think of them as being anything else. They have truly been a miracle and second chance for all of us. They have changed us for the better, and have made our lives complete. They are adored beyond measure by their siblings, "Mema, Sissy, and Bubba Will." They have given Brandi the miracle of being a full-time mama to not one baby but two, and she never has to share them! (Remember, God often gives us exactly what we ask for!)

And me? He has given me a second chance to be a daddy. Our hearts are full and our family is complete.

And just in case you are wondering, we need nothing else that breathes in this house, including four-legged ones.

Being in our forties, having five children ranging in ages from two to seventeen, one of whom has severe autism, and owning our own business which requires travel, we get the question a lot, "How do you all do it?"

I often reply, "How do you not?" I am not trying to be a jerk, but knowing everything you know so far, really how do you not? In everything we have done in our lives, we have felt it was what God had called us to do.

Just like Will and his autism. Is it is easy? No. Do we feel that what the enemy meant for evil God has turned to good? Without a doubt. Anyone who knows Will, has met him or has read about him can't help but love him. It is no secret he is a special young man and God has a special place in his heart for him. In the same regard, I have no question that this path was meant for us to walk with all five of our children. We can't help but know God ordained this even before he made that promise to Brandi.

Having two young ones later in life is a challenge, for sure. Are the days hard? Yes. Are the nights long? Yes. Are the struggles real? Yes. But the rewards are beyond anything I can explain or comprehend.

I'm just so thankful for what God has done in all our lives and what he is continuing to do. In our wildest dreams, we could have never imagined how God would make difficult situations into a miraculous ones. He can take nothing and all of a sudden make the impossible come true. We have to believe and be patient. God always has a plan. Having patience is not an easy thing for any of us, especially when we are "waiting" for something or wanting something. But I can tell you from experience to keep moving, keep going, no matter how long because God will give you your Chance and he will make a Myracle out of what you thought was impossible.

12
THAT DAY

This may seem like a strange ending to this book, but bear with me. It was a hot day that early July morning as I prepared for my second day of crisis management training in south Arkansas. I had stayed with my parents the night before as I do often when working in the area. It is a win-win in many ways. It allows me to spend time with them, cuts down on drive time, allows me to miss the traffic of a long commute and helps me make it to my class on time. I have found over the years that it really helps to be on time when you are the instructor.

I eagerly gathered all my belongings, excited that the end of the week had arrived and I would be going home by the end of the day. I was more than ready to see my wife and spend time with her and the kids for the weekend before heading back out on Sunday. My older girls were home, too, for their summer break and we had great plans.

With the weekend in mind, I had a little extra pep in my step. I said goodbye to my parents, loaded my car, and set off. The air that morning was thick. It was hot! One of those

Arkansas July mornings when it was hot enough to make you sweat walking from the house to the car as early as 7 am.

With the air conditioning blowing full blast, I headed out. The highway running beside my parents' home was not busy at all which was pretty normal on any given morning. I pulled out with ease and headed to the main highway. I was in very familiar territory. I had lived in this area of Arkansas most of my life and knew the roads like the back of my hand. Probably I could have driven them with my eyes closed. For the time of day it was, I was surprised traffic was as light as it was, contributing it to being the end of a holiday week for many. I saw an occasional truck pulling a boat and figured many people were still off work or vacationing.

I had been on the road for a couple miles before making a quick stop through the drive through for a breakfast sandwich. I was listening to one of my favorite stations on the radio and was making good time. With it being summer and all the kids at home, I had chosen not to call. I knew they were probably all still asleep and didn't want to take the chance of waking any of them. So unlike many mornings, I didn't call Brandi. I knew I would see her that afternoon and would try to call and catch her during one of my breaks or at lunch.

As I drove thinking about my day, the class I was teaching, and the weekend ahead I was full of anticipation for what the day held. I loved my job. Friday's are the best day of the week and I was getting to spend the weekend with all five of my children, so it couldn't have been a better day.

But as I rounded a corner, a corner I had driven my entire life, at the normal rate of speed, the unexpected occurred. In a strange turn of events, I realized I had gotten too far on the edge of the road. Panic set in. I did what many others would do under those circumstances—I tried to correct by turning the steering wheel quickly to the left. The result was more like a jerk to get my car, a Mitsubishi Gallant, back on the road.

Within seconds, I realized that maneuver had not worked

like it was intended. My car slid straight ahead instead of going to the left as expected. Referring back to all the safety courses, defensive driving class and years of driving experience, I began to turn it again, working to correct the wheels and get them back on the road.

Despite my best efforts, experience and training, I pulled too far back to the right and found myself with a wheel off of the road. As in any emergency situation, you almost feel as though you are having an out of body experience. You realize everything is happening within a few short seconds, but at the time it seems like it is in slow motion and that you have all the time in the world you need, until sheer panic sets in.

As I assessed my environment and what I should do next, thoughts came flooding to my mind—not necessarily my life flashing before my eyes, but perhaps less important things. I looked up to be greeted by the side of the guardrail, and before I could do anything, I hit it on the driver side of the car.

The next several minutes are still a blank, but as I awoke, I found myself in a daze on the side of the hill surrounded by several people I thought had to be angels.

Oh my! Here we go again! More miracles and more second chances!